HOLY WARRIORS

HOLY WARRIORS

The Abolitionists and American Slavery

Revised Edition

JAMES BREWER STEWART

CONSULTING EDITOR: ERIC FONER

HILL AND WANG

A division of Farrar, Straus and Giroux
New York

LIBRARY OF CONGRESS CATALOGING-IN-PUBLICATION DATA
Stewart, James Brewer.
Holy warriors : the abolitionists and American slavery / James
Brewer Stewart ; consulting editor, Eric Foner. — Rev. ed., 1st ed.
    p.   cm.
Includes bibliographical references (p.) and index.
ISBN 0-8090-1596-X (paper : alk. paper)
    1. Antislavery movements — United States.   I. Foner, Eric.   II. Title.
E446.S83   1996
326 — dc20   96-33260
                                               CIP

ACKNOWLEDGMENTS

The publication of *Holy Warriors* in 1976 was followed by a slow but ever more massive avalanche of scholarship on the abolitionist movement. Responding critically to its enormity in a revision that, I hope, retains brevity, focus, and accessibility has proven an invigorating challenge. Fortunately, many people who represent exactly the readerships for which this new version is intended were willing to assist me. I wish to thank them all:

Arthur Wang and Eric Foner are without peers as critics and colleagues. Without their continuing support and understanding, neither the original volume nor this revision would have been possible.

As I revised, several dozen talented Macalester College undergraduates criticized the drafts, much improving both style and content. One student in particular, Carissa Baquiran, made fundamental interpretive suggestions.

Two members of my family share a genetic aversion to bad writing. Without their essential help, I would still be struggling for control over my manuscript:

My daughter, Rebecca, an editorial virtuoso, rooted out all manner of stylistic infelicity, saved me from embarrassing pomposities, and forced me to sharpen my focus at every turn.

Over three decades, my wife, Dottie, has encountered my prose at its ugliest, my logic at its worst, and my organization at its most chaotic. In my scholarship (as in so many more important matters) she continues, lovingly, to help me to think again.

96197

TO MY MOTHER AND FATHER

CONTENTS

HOLY WARRIORS

PREFACE:
SLAVERY IN REPUBLICAN AMERICA

In January 1863, as war raged between North and South, Wendell Phillips addressed an audience of over ten thousand in Brooklyn, New York. His listeners pressed forward as this grandiloquent radical orator, "abolitionism's golden trumpet," spoke of the war's deeper significance. "It is to be a long fight," Phillips advised, "only one part of a great fight going on the world over, and which began ages ago . . . between free institutions and caste institutions, Freedom and Democracy against institutions of privilege and class." The crowd roared its approval.

There was considerable truth in Phillips's remark. One hundred years before Phillips spoke, hereditary systems of inequality had dominated most of Western Europe and the New World. Few had questioned the rights of aristocratic families in Europe and England to command the labor of villeins and serfs. Rarely had people expressed distress that France, England, Spain, Portugal, and Holland presided over rich American empires based on the enslavement of black Africans. For centuries, Western Europeans had accepted the axiom that a properly ordered society respected local privileges, deprecated economic individualism, and had no place for cosmopolitan ideas about human equality. But in the century before Wendell Phillips spoke in Brooklyn, all these things had changed dramatically.

In 1811, the year of Phillips's birth, slavery had been all but abolished in the Northern United States. In his lifetime, he witnessed emancipation in practically every part of Latin America. He also observed the complex process by which states in Western Europe discarded traditional inequality for newer democratic forms by abandoning peasant labor and expanding the common man's political rights. And just twenty days before this gathering in Brooklyn, President Abraham Lincoln had issued the Emancipation Proclamation, declaring that slaves in the rebel states must be considered free.

Whatever the forces behind this enormous transformation, the abolition of slavery in the United States was central to the process. British North Americans, after all, had been the first to insist that all men are created equal. Yet by the 1840s the Southern United States had become the most formidable slave economy in the Western world, and the federal government had evolved into a defender of slaveholders' interests in domestic politics and international affairs. But by 1863 Phillips would predict to his audience that "the South is to be annihilated," that the slaveholding "aristocracy of the skin which considers the Declaration of Independence a sham and democracy a snare" was about to be obliterated. As Phillips was fully aware, one of the last and most powerful examples of an older order, established in the days of Europe's seventeenth-century empires, was finally being eclipsed by a more modern and dynamic society.

Before the American Revolution, Wendell Phillips's father could never have anticipated this outcome, so prominent had slavery been in the world economy of his day. On British- and French-held Caribbean islands as well as in Spanish and Portuguese colonies throughout Latin America, cohesive slaveowning classes and immense numbers of blacks produced staggering amounts of sugar, tobacco, coffee, and rum, as well as a treasure of precious metals. The African slave trade, stimulated by booming profits, had itself expanded into an intensely competitive enterprise. By the 1770s, Africans by the hundreds of thousands were being used to turn many parts of the "new world" into plantation societies. The thirteen British colonies on the North American mainland were no exception. Even as they were declaring their own independence, every colony, North and South, maintained some form of black slavery.

In colonial New England the use of slaves was common, but subject to extreme regional variation. Rural New Englanders seldom had any need for slave labor. By the beginning of the eighteenth century, however, in Rhode Island, New York, New Jersey, Pennsylvania, and Delaware, slavery was being profitably pursued on large farms in the countryside. Slaves also applied their energies to urban manufacturing enterprises as skilled artisans and day laborers. In New York City, Philadelphia, and Boston in particular, urban slaves comprised a large percentage of growing black communities which were to provide important leadership in the struggle against slavery. But slaveholding was never essential to the colonial North's economy of freehold farming, trade, and local manufacturing. During the eighteenth century, the number of Northern blacks, free or enslaved, was fewer than sixty thousand — no more than four percent of the white population. Thus, in the North emancipation could be accomplished with a minimum of conflict.

In the South, far different circumstances prevailed. From the Maryland and Virginia tidewater to the Georgia frontier, slavery influenced nearly every aspect of the region's colonial development. English colonists everywhere proved willing exploiters of slave labor, but those who established slavery in the Southern colonies also developed a distinctive culture which contrasted sharply with that of the North.

The beginning of Southern slavery was more accidental than premeditated. The earliest white settlers harbored no aspirations of becoming slave masters, but they carried with them deep prejudices against people with dark skin. These biases, which sprang from a combination of religious preoccupation, aesthetic preferences, and cultural predilections, were reinforced by the growing need for unskilled labor among whites on the southern frontier. In a system initially based in white indentured servitude, ambitious English settlers put highest premium on commanding the labor of people of any race or geographic origin who had "forfeited" their right to work for themselves. African people, first imported to Virginia and Maryland as unwilling workers but not as legally defined slaves, quickly came to serve as particularly compelling objects of negative self-definition for English settlers as they attempted to make sense of their puzzling new circumstances. The Africans' blackness, symbolizing sin, affirmed by visual contrast the English colonists' sanctified self-image as "white" people. Soon a cycle of debasement and exploitation took hold. By the end of the seventeenth century, black laborers in Virginia and Maryland found themselves turned by law into hereditary slaves as English settlers throughout the colonies molded their perceptions of blackness and whiteness into rigid categories that sorted people of differing skin colors into "races." Henceforth, most whites would simply assume that "the blacks" had always existed as a race apart. That particular historical circumstances accounted for these ideas, not unchanging, God-given "facts," was a truth that few whites ever questioned.

Spanish and Portuguese colonists in the Caribbean demonstrated just how lucrative plantation slavery could be, and the institution spread rapidly throughout Georgia and the Carolinas. As the eighteenth century opened, slavery seemed to Southern colonists the absolute prerequisite for order, liberty, and prosperity, since the system of black labor guaranteed that

large planters would never be faced with a rebellious population of lower-class whites. White freedom, in this important
sense, had come to depend on black slavery. At the time of the
American Revolution, a full thirty-five out of every hundred
Southern inhabitants were of African ancestry; blacks accounted for thirty to forty percent of those living in Maryland,
Virginia, and North Carolina. In some coastal areas of colonial
South Carolina, blacks outnumbered whites by as much as five
to one as natural increases among settled slaves and continuous
infusions from Africa were easily absorbed by the burgeoning
cash-crop system.

As English and African settlers interacted with each other
on a daily basis, they began to create a truly distinctive biracial
culture. Despite harsh new categories of race that developed
in the minds of white colonists, extensive blendings of African
and English elements resulted in new patterns of language,
religious expression, architecture, folk art, cuisine, work patterns, codes of manners and morality, and especially the
growth of a "mixed race" population. In this fundamental respect, the South, not the North, was always the more racially
integrated society, a fact that only intensified slaveholders' anger when abolitionists assailed their moral conduct. The high
percentage of blacks in the rural population also made it possible for slaves to create autonomous communities that masters
were never wholly able to control. On larger plantations especially, this margin of autonomy, centered in the slave quarters, sustained the slaves' will to resist and to protect one
another, as well as their masters' belief that black slaves were
indeed a "troublesome property."

The pervasive presence of slave laborers also led to complex
and important relationships among whites. Every Southern colony prior to the Revolution contained elite groups of large
slaveholders, often related by marriage, who dominated the
political process, controlled the economy, and defined social

norms. In Virginia and Maryland, no less than in South Carolina and Georgia, none could doubt the success of opulent "first families" in establishing political supremacy on the basis of their scores of slaves and thousands of acres. Aristocratic in bearing, taste, and outlook, the wealthy eighteenth-century planters set the pattern for the next generation of slaveholders, who felt driven to oppose radical abolitionists like Wendell Phillips. These rural magnates retained dominion by exercising the prerogative of lineage and inherited status. In their society, egalitarian concepts such as "individualism," "democracy," and "equality" were subordinate to the dictates of local custom. The world of the planter depended on a clear ordering of unequals — proud over humble, rich over poor, male over female, and white over black — all of which nurtured powerful expectations of mastery and obedience.

To some extent, the lives of all whites throughout Southern society were influenced by the planter elites. From the Revolution until the Civil War, small slaveowners, non-slaveowning farmers, and poorer whites constituted a majority of the South's white population, and within this broad sector there was great variation. Prosperous farmers, often of Quaker, German, and Scotch–Irish descent, usually chose to settle in the upper South, apart from the large plantations. In Delaware, eastern Maryland, northern and eastern Virginia, and elsewhere, family farming and commercial activity, not slave-based planting, constituted the primary economic activity. Removed from the planters' dominance, these freeholders prized the virtues of self-reliance as they established small towns and farmsteads where free blacks also preferred to settle. In such areas, there soon evolved a potentially subversive "middle ground," where slavery was legal but where many citizens nurtured the values of free labor. To the increasing distress of planter elites, disagreements over slavery would always exist in these middle-ground areas, undercutting the possibility of a white South united to protect its "peculiar institution." In the Deep South, where large planters held preeminence, antislavery dissent was not possible within the white majority. The planters controlled desirable farmlands, and ambitious freeholders found it difficult to rise in society. Instead, they emulated their "betters" by cultivating smaller plots, perhaps with the help of one or two slaves. Some of these enterprises supported prosperous ways of life. Other small slaveholders spent a lifetime scratching out barely viable existences. In either case, marginal slaveholders and poor whites added significantly to the customs of inequality in plantation society. For the most part, the lesser whites felt deep affinities with the elite planters and regarded their economic dominance with jealous awe. There were class tensions and hostilities between and within families, but complex blood ties between slaveholders large and small counterbalanced them. The planter's sense of noblesse oblige toward his "inferiors," black and white alike, built on such ties and further bound the classes together.

Undergirding these social patterns of the plantation South was the primary relationship between masters and slaves, as individuals and as groups. Long before 1776, the identities of all people in the Deep South, black and white, rich and poor, were shaped by the tensions between ownership and bondage, privilege and exploitation, resentment and gratitude, patriarchy and dependence, resistance and obedience, and, above all, blackness and whiteness. Given this pervasive interaction, all proposals for emancipation were met with implacable hostility from every stratum of the white population. By 1776, the Virginia tobacco elites, the Carolina lowland squires, and many lesser whites had come to share a profoundly ironic fate. Long before republican colonists demanded independence from England and proclaimed all men equal, slavery had come to

supply whites in the Deep South with the fundamental under-
pinning of their way of life.

In the midst of the Civil War, Wendell Phillips no longer
found it useful to dwell on these inconsistencies. For years he
had protested his fellow citizens' eagerness simultaneously to
applaud democracy and to condone slavery, but with slavery
now so close to extinction, these points seemed irrelevant. Reflecting instead on emancipation and the war that had brought
it about, Phillips remarked to his Brooklyn audience that "our
Revolution began in 1775 and never [since] was the country
left in peace." Regarding the problem of slavery, there was
considerable justification for his statement. In the late colonial
period, the dramatic, often violent processes that led to the
Civil War had first dismantled slave empires in the "New
World." In tracing abolition back to America's revolutionary
origins, Phillips could not have been more accurate.

1

ABOLITION IN THE AGE
OF REVOLUTION

"We expect great things from men who have made such a noble stand against the designs of their *fellow-men* to enslave them." So declared Sambo Freeman, Peter Bestes, and two other slaves in 1773 in their petition to the Massachusetts Assembly to grant them their freedom. Theirs was an especially pointed comment, since at that very moment Massachusetts legislators were vocally condemning the British for acts of "enslavement." For more than a century, British North Americans had felt little discomfort over treating people as possessions. But on the eve of the American Revolution, as Freeman and Bestes's petition suggests, the debate between Great Britain and her colonies was also inspiring unprecedented attacks on slavery. The inconsistency between Patrick Henry's demand to "Give me liberty or give me death" and his ownership of over a hundred slaves seemed increasingly difficult to justify.

To be sure, earlier generations of colonists had not been wholly without antislavery spokesmen. Before the eighteenth century, small Quaker communities and isolated Puritan theologians had agonized over the conflict between holding slaves and trying to live "by the light of Divine Truth." But such expressions had never before evoked a broad response. On the eve of the Revolution, however, many Quakers were freeing their slaves, and even some of the South's leading planters were practicing gradual emancipation. Politicians all over the colonies spoke against the horrors of the African slave trade and many abolition societies petitioned governments to enact emancipation bills and to ease restrictions against individual manumissions. All over the colonies, slaves like Freeman and Bestes were purchasing, petitioning, and suing for freedom. Planters in the South suspected that they were losing control over their slaves, who seemed unusually inclined to escape or even to organize resistance. By the 1790s, legislation for the gradual elimination of slavery was being enacted or considered in every Northern state. As African Americans well understood, the patriots' struggle for national independence had, from its inception, begun to undermine the legitimacy of owning slaves.

Two powerful ideological forces inspired the Revolution, and both gave rise to unprecedented attacks on slavery. The first of these, the political ideas of the European Enlightenment, led patriots such as Thomas Jefferson to justify their revolution as an expression of natural law. According to this political philosophy, rational humans could understand the workings of nature unaided by divine revelation and could act decisively to eradicate tyranny, cultivate freedom, and promote social progress. No longer believing that humans were dominated by Original Sin or manipulated by a capricious God, people influenced by such thinking were freed to question traditional Christian justifications for slavery, seeing them as untenable "superstition" or as relics of a "barbarian" age.

Enlightenment ideas by no means led automatically to antislavery conclusions, as was demonstrated by Jefferson's lifelong unwillingness to free his slaves. The strong emphasis on protecting private property in Enlightenment thought could also be used to argue against emancipation, as could the rationalist view that prevailing customs usually represented improvements on the past. Yet when patriots insisted that the dictates of reason compelled their struggle for freedom, the continued submission of slaves to their masters became much more difficult to defend on logical grounds. Slaves, for their part, eagerly assimilated their masters' preference for "liberty," to make their own claims. Sambo Freeman and Peter Bestes spoke for countless slaves when petitioning for emancipation on the grounds of Enlightenment principles. Henceforward, slaves and free blacks invariably invoked "natural law" when asserting their rights.

Protestant evangelicalism was a second, at least as powerful as secular thinking in making ordinary Americans question the morality of slaveowning. Common people had borne witness to explosive religious feelings well before the beginning of the conflict with England. As they did so, they discovered religious sensibilities that were soon to lead the Revolution in antislavery directions. During the 1730s and 1740s, Americans grew accustomed to calling the religious upheavals around them the Great Awakening. Deeply troubled by fears of religious backsliding, by alienation from the life-styles of the upper classes, and by fear of encroaching materialism, many ordinary colonists, black as well as white, gave vent to their anxieties through expressions of emotional pietism.

The result was an upheaval of evangelical feeling and an unprecedented mingling of Christians of both races in the first of a series of religious revivals which were to extend well into the nineteenth century. The itinerant preachers of the Great Awakening stressed several aspects of traditional Christianity: most notably, humanity's sinful nature and God's wrathful judgment. They did so while attempting to inspire their listeners into the ecstatic experience of "conversion," a sudden communion with God during which a person was spiritually cleansed and reborn into a life of Christian dedication. In England and in every American colony, thousands of anxious souls embraced "conversion," uplifted by the sermons of powerful preachers like George Whitefield, Jonathan Edwards, and William Tennent.

The crucial point was that people began to see themselves as doing their own choosing, now believing that sin and salvation were not arbitrarily predetermined by an unknowable God. Instead, people were free to trust their religious feelings, to embrace salvation, and to live according to the dictates of Christian morality. It was a formula which denied humanity's enslavement to sin, dramatized the value of impulsive personal commitment, and demanded that people take responsibility for their own and their fellow Christians' day-to-day actions. At the same time, revivalism fostered unprecedented spiritual inclusiveness, especially in the South, where common people of both races prayed, sang, and shouted together, scorning the staid Anglicanism of their slaveholding "betters." Such practices clearly documented the subversive character of this religious impulse which, for a time, placed black and white together in the Christian community. A God who granted everyone the choice of salvation could set little store by race or status.

While white revival ministers hoped to bring the slaves the spiritual freedom of God's Word, not physical liberation from their masters, the deepest significance of evangelicalism for abolitionism lay elsewhere, in the feelings of the converts themselves. Among slaves and free blacks, the Great Awakening called forth powerful lay preachers whose messages of hope sustained the slave community and whose powerful oratory established enduring modes of expression for African American activists. By placing the voice of conscience over law, free will over original sin, and mutual benevolence over divine retribution, many Protestants, white no less than black, began groping toward a new vision of spiritual and personal liberty.

First to act upon the antislavery implications of intuitive religion were the Quakers. From the beginning, Quakers stressed the absolute universality of God's love, the brotherhood of man, the sinfulness of physical coercion. Such beliefs led some early Quakers, including the religion's founder, George Fox, to conclude in the 1670s that holding slaves violated God's fundamental precepts. So convinced, these early radicals began to remonstrate with their slaveowning colleagues, arguing that to obey the "inner light" meant taking responsibility for the "oppressed African." In the minds of these Quaker abolitionists, slaveowning was a moral abomination identical to theft, a crime further compounded by adultery, since slave dealing separated wives and husbands. Demanding that their slaveowning brethren repent, emancipate, and endorse abolition, antislavery-minded Quakers also shuddered at the implications of slave insurrections for their pacifist creed. As one Friend queried: "Have these Negroes not as much right to fight for their freedom as you have to keep them slaves?"

Other exceptional Friends found themselves impelled to strive for abolition. Hunchbacked Benjamin Lay, for example, had lived for a time in Barbados as a slaveholder before settling in Pennsylvania in 1731. His experience as a master had left him tortured by the guilty memory of flogging helpless slaves whom he had accused of stealing. For the rest of his life, Lay sought atonement by challenging the apathy of fellow Quakers with theatrical displays, such as spraying a surprised audience with "slaves' blood" made from pokeberry squeezings. With less flamboyance and greater success, John Woolman traveled the Southern middle ground in the 1740s and 1750s, capitalizing on the "great revival" by persuading receptive planters in Virginia, Delaware, and Maryland to manumit their slaves. But Quarterly and Yearly Meetings of Quakers usually paid scant attention to dissenters such as these. Until the mid-eighteenth century, abolitionism remained a minority position.

Many Friends continued to hold slaves, and leading Quakers in Pennsylvania and Rhode Island remained deeply engaged in the West African slave trade. The Quaker majority transformed itself into a crusade against slaveowning only when faced with a sudden denominational crisis. During the mid-1750s, pacifist Quakers who controlled the Pennsylvania Assembly refused to support colonial wars against the French and their Indian allies, a moral dilemma that became so intense that the Pennsylvania Friends withdrew from colonial government. Their decision meant abandoning William Penn's "holy experiment" of a Quaker-directed Commonwealth and led them to an agonizing search for the source of their tribulations. Sensitive to the currents of the Great Awakening, they concluded that reformation required a revival of religious feeling, and they called on one another to rededicate themselves to the unadorned dictates of the "inner light." As a result, Quarterly Meetings grew increasingly receptive to John Woolman, Anthony Benezet, and others whose preaching traced the Friends' trials to their involvement with slavery. The widespread acceptance of such assertions by Pennsylvania's Friends next began to involve them in a transatlantic movement, for in England their fellow Quakers had launched a far-flung antislavery crusade.

On both sides of the Atlantic, Quaker antislavery was inextricably linked to entrepreneurial families whose fortunes were made from shipping, banking, mining, and insurance. No other eighteenth-century group more fully typified the rising tempo of transatlantic commercialism. In America, for example, leading Quaker families in Newport, Rhode Island, built fortunes in the Caribbean import-export market (a commercial network dominated by products of slave labor), and Moses Brown of Philadelphia served as a director of the first Bank of the United States. Whether in London, Birmingham, New York, or Philadelphia, Quakers had come to embody and stimulate the forces of cosmopolitan commercial capitalism. In all spheres of activity, they strove for social efficiency, economic progress, moral benevolence, and civic-mindedness. Though these values could as easily support slavery as question it, they took on strong abolitionist overtones when infused with an inclusive religious evangelicalism. To evangelical Quakers, abolitionism was only a part, albeit a crucial part, of God's broader plan for human progress. Incorporating banks, issuing stock, founding hospitals, converting unbelievers, or manumitting slaves — all helped to build a morally ordered, spiritually revitalized society. Oppressed slaves were to be transformed into pious, upright workers. Indolent masters were to learn sobriety, thrift, and moral responsibility. Thus, while British Quakers busied themselves opposing England's slave-based interests in the West Indies, American Friends worked toward emancipation in the mainland colonies.

Ultimately, international Quakerism exerted a powerful antislavery influence over the crucial 1758 Yearly Meeting. Here, over the opposition of slaveowning Friends, Benezet and Woolman argued successfully for a condemnation not only of the foreign and domestic slave trade but also of slavery itself. As English Quakers added a stinging indictment, the Philadelphia Meeting voted to exclude from positions of authority any members who bought or sold slaves. Henceforth, proslavery Quakers were unable to dominate the Society. Official committees were deputed at once to impress slaveholding Quakers with the imperative of emancipation. By the end of the Revolution, it was practically impossible to locate a Quaker living north of Virginia who dealt in slaves. Three decades of efforts at self-reform had achieved impressive results. But success brought no feelings of complacency; it dictated instead that Quakers carry the battle out of the meeting house and into the larger society.

During the 1760s and 1770s, as alienation deepened between

patriots and Parliament, exponents of religious evangelism and Enlightenment rationalism both drew closer to the Quakers' crusade. Ever more sensitive to encroachments on their traditional privileges, patriots constantly warned that oppressive English officials were conspiring to overthrow natural law and to subject them to slavery. Rationalists such as Benjamin Franklin and Thomas Paine quoted Locke, Montesquieu, and English libertarian writers as they sought to preserve American liberties against "corrupt" England's exercise of arbitrary power. Biblicists like the Reverend Jonathan Mayhew preached that British "enslavement" represented the righteous judgments of an angry God upon His wayward American children. In the context of revolutionary thought, patriots thus freighted the concept of slavery with profound significance. When colonists employed the term "slavery" with reference to English policy, they meant the destruction of a person's property, inherent liberties, even one's personal preference for freedom. Political slavery reminded them of Old World despotisms like Turkey, Russia, and ultimately even England itself. Across the globe, as they saw it, rational, free men and sanctified Christians were in danger of being transformed into superstitious, enervated serfs dominated by impious, corrupt lords. Viewed in this manner, America appeared to the patriots quite literally the last refuge of freedom.

The excruciating contrast between their own claims of liberty and the powerlessness of the slaves became simply too obvious for some patriots to ignore. From the first, their protests contained abolitionist overtones. As early as 1764, the influential James Otis of Massachusetts pondered this problem in Enlightenment terms, and his conclusions anticipated by a decade phrases which were to be commonplace on the eve of independence. Denouncing slavery as "a most shocking violation of the law of nature," a practice which "makes every dealer a tyrant," Otis denied that "any logical inference in favor of slavery" could be drawn "from a flat nose, a long or a short face." He concluded by warning that not all threats to American liberty came from abroad. Slaveholders, "who every day barter away other men's liberty," would soon "care little for their own," Otis asserted, and would plunge government into "ferocity, cruelty and brutal barbarity." Slaveowning not only compromised the patriots' defense of American rights but threatened to subvert their liberties from within.

As relations with England dissolved into warfare, many other leaders began to follow Otis's rationalist thinking, linking antislavery with the patriots' cause. Patrick Henry, John Adams, Alexander Hamilton, Thomas Paine, Albert Gallatin, James Madison, Thomas Jefferson, and many other luminaries declared slavery a dangerous contravention of the Revolution's aims. Hamilton, Gallatin, and Benjamin Franklin became particularly active in manumissionist circles. To be sure, not all these individuals were as convinced as Otis had been that environmental influences, not innate qualities, accounted for the disturbing "differences" perceived in black people by so many whites. Jefferson, for one, struggled in vain to square his rationalist's commitment to environmental explanations of human differences with his gnawing "suspicion" that blacks were by nature brutal and intellectually shallow. Yet the major significance of these espousals was that abolitionism, expressed as Enlightenment philosophy, was now proving influential in powerful circles of national politics.

While justifying revolution as fulfilling "natural law," leading patriots also rekindled the spirit of the Great Awakening. Among New England Calvinists, revolutionary turmoil evoked apocalyptic responses that inextricably linked the trials of the nation with the torments of the sinner. Revivalists exhorted that liberty could never be preserved from the British, God's instrument of retribution, until citizens had cast out their collective enslavement to worldliness and disbelief. Extending these concepts of slavery and freedom further still, many New England evangelicals began vocally to oppose the enslavement of blacks as the foulest of the nation's transgressions, the principal obstacle to realizing independence. The differences between rationalist politicians and evangelical exhorters blurred as both emphasized the importance of abolition for the securing of independence. Calvinist luminaries like the Reverend Samuel Hopkins spoke out, joining Quakers such as Benezet and Woolman, Methodists like Francis Asbury, and deists like Benjamin Franklin and Thomas Paine. It was a formidable coalition, at least in the North, which prepared the Revolution's thrust for emancipation.

Above all, it was the pervasive influence of warfare itself that led Americans to further the cause of abolition. While exhorting their white parishioners to arms, evangelical ministers could hardly counsel submissiveness among the slaves. Yet at the same time these ministers feared that a retributive God would visit black insurrection as well as British victories on sinful Americans unless they freed their slaves. In 1775 such prophecies appeared well-nigh fulfilled when Lord Dunmore, Virginia's Royal Governor, promised freedom to all slaves who would desert rebellious masters and serve in the King's army. Over eight hundred black royalists enlisted, giving substance to Hopkins's warning that God was "so ordering it in his Providence" to induce the slaves "to take up arms against us . . . in order to get their liberty." By the estimate of historian Benjamin Quarles, nearly twenty thousand escaped to the British side during the course of the war.

Still larger numbers of slaves exploited the confusion of warfare to secure their freedom as Americans. Throughout the "middle ground," as well as in Philadelphia, Boston, and New York, slave artisans hired out to other whites by absent masters took advantage of their relative independence to quietly slip away into free black communities. In the Southern countryside, at least ten thousand slaves escaped to Spanish or French settlements, made their ways to Indian villages, or fled to the North. The ranks of the newly emancipated swelled further when difficulties in obtaining white volunteers led several Northern legislatures to grant freedom to slaves who fought in the militia. In Maryland, masters were also induced with guarantees of compensation to enlist and emancipate their slaves. As in every subsequent American war, many whites could not stifle their feelings of guilt as blacks gave their lives in defense of the society that so thoroughly oppressed them. Support for emancipation became the obvious way to make amends.

Blacks in every part of the North responded to these unparalleled opportunities with growing sophistication. While prominent black heroes such as Crispus Attucks and Prince Hall supplied stirring examples of patriotism to white and blacks alike, less famous free blacks found themselves thrust by the Revolution into positions of leadership. Young James Forten contrived his escape in 1779 from a notorious British prison ship in which he was held captive, and was changed forever by the experience. Convinced henceforth that the Revolution "required the overthrow of all distinctions of color," Forten went on to become one of Philadelphia's wealthiest businessmen, most generous philanthropists, most active abolitionists, and most forceful agents of community empowerment.

In this climate of growing activism, those still enslaved also expressed newly politicized views of their rights. A slave known to us only as Prince conveyed to the 1777 Massachusetts Assembly a petition for emancipation on behalf of "A Great Number of Blacks detained in a State of slavery in the Bowels of a free and Christian Country." In 1779, the Connecticut General Assembly received a similar statement from Negroes living in Fairfield County. Another group of enslaved petitioners likewise insisted that "Every Principle from which

America has acted in the course of its difficulties with Great Britain pleads stronger than a thousand arguments" for emancipation.

The free blacks who joined slaves in petition campaigns and sued in court on behalf of those still in bondage testified to the dramatic transformation of Northern African American communities that was being wrought by the Revolution. Henceforth, in Boston, New York, Philadelphia, and other Northern cities, free blacks would offer leadership crucial to abolitionism while strengthening their neighborhoods in the face of continuing discrimination. By 1780, for example, the black citizens of Providence, Rhode Island, had founded their own benevolent association, designed to assist the unemployed and those dislocated by personal reversals. By the mid-1790s, aggressive black leaders in every large Northern city had built on precedents like this to create an impressive range of aid societies, fraternal orders, benevolent groups, churches, and private schools.

With antislavery activism and national patriotism now so fully intertwined, slavery slowly began to unravel throughout the North. In 1774, Quakers led by Anthony Benezet bombarded the Continental Congress with antislavery demands and finally obtained its consent to stop all slave importations. The following year, Philadelphia Quakers organized the first association devoted exclusively to abolition, the Society for the Relief of Free Negroes Unlawfully Held in Bondage. Sympathetic to the Quaker zeal for useful improvements in the name of economic progress, powerful politicians, manufacturing magnates, and lawyers — the dynamic commercial and professional sectors of Northern society — likewise took up the abolitionist cause. Only a few of these urban entrepreneurs owned slaves, and very few of the North's significant men of wealth depended on slavery for social position or economic advancement. Slaves also were too few to pose a serious threat to white supremacy once they had been granted their freedom. Social harmony and economic betterment would be enhanced, leading whites maintained, once emancipation removed motives for rebellion. The impressive programs of self-education and moral uplift now being undertaken by Northern free blacks deepened these impressions considerably.

Under these circumstances, the forces of abolitionism proved irresistible in the end. By 1784, every Northern state save New York and New Jersey had enacted laws providing for gradual emancipation; by 1804, these two states, too, had passed such bills. Of course, racism and the economic interest of slaveholders generated stubborn obstruction. Northern abolition, moreover, led always to segregation and denials of political rights and terrible moments of violent white racism, not to genuine equality. Yet, for the only time in American history, abolitionists black and white had succeeded in peacefully merging with those who controlled the levers of power. Elsewhere, without such impressive institutional support, their pleas evoked much less willing responses. Ultimately, in most of the Revolutionary South, abolition made no headway at all.

For slaveholders throughout the South, the Revolution created enormous problems. No less receptive than Northerners to the Revolution's antislavery overtones, many planters became genuinely disturbed by slavery's moral implications. Yet as slaves made the Revolution their own by fleeing, fighting, and signing emancipation petitions, masters also began to fear for their fundamental authority. Many of their bondspeople were proving disconcertingly well informed and capable of concerted effort, dangerous tendencies even in tranquil times. Among middle-ground non-slaveholders, as well as throughout the North, antislavery feelings expressed themselves ever more widely. Yet, whatever the planter's private worries, his own financial and psychological dependence on the slavery system remained as total as ever.

Beset by conflicting preoccupations, leading planters did not embrace abolitionism, but instead a commitment to humanize slavery. Barbarous punishments, they declared, should be abandoned and prohibitions on private emancipations eased. Masters should be kindly, paternal figures to their slaves, avoiding if possible displays of raw power. Castration and other forms of mutilation as punishment were written out of the slave codes, replaced by provisos making it a crime for masters to grossly mistreat their slaves. Jefferson, Madison, and other notables supported easing restrictions on voluntary emancipation, and some large slaveholders such as George Washington made complicated provisions for the gradual release of their bondsmen as each satisfied certain "fitness" requirements.

But by attempting by these means to reform slavery, the planters added mightily to the very problems they were attempting to solve. Most crucially, the large number of private emancipations stimulated by their efforts insured the rapid expansion of the one population group in the region that planters distrusted most. By 1810, thanks to voluntary manumissions, the number of free blacks living in the slave states had ballooned to well over a hundred thousand. Because of the stringent requirements of their emancipation agreements, many of these freedpeople were literate and highly skilled, possessing a cosmopolitan outlook, leadership potential, and clear ideas about their rights.

Especially in northern Virginia, Delaware, and Maryland, where freehold farming and commercial activity were now expanding at the expense of slave-produced tobacco, the danger of antislavery collaboration between free blacks and freehold whites quickly became obvious to worried planters. Sensing these tensions, Quakers spoke with enthusiasm to economically hard-pressed upper-South slaveholders about the logic of emancipation. Every characteristic that made the upper South suspect to slaveholders and so important to abolitionists had now been established — falling tobacco and slave prices, exhausted soil, discouraged planters, active communities of free blacks and antislavery-minded whites, and, above all, the close proximity of the free states, whose influence favored the southward expansion of free labor. These areas of the upper South, it must be emphasized, were hardly a racial utopia. Throughout the decades, the ambiguous boundaries between freed and enslaved generated dangerous racial tensions and often provoked violent outbursts from insecure whites. But despite its conformity to dominant racial norms, the middle ground represented an expanding worry for planters farther south.

In the Deep South, slavery retained its supremacy, for it proved an exceptionally adaptable system even in the age of revolution. Contrary to older historical opinions, in the rice-growing parts of the Carolinas and Georgia, as well as in rich tobacco lands in lower Virginia and western Maryland, slavery was hardly dying in the years just after 1776. Here, prices and profits remained stable as rich planters amassed new credit that underwrote substantial expansions of acreage. The loss of British protection, though serious, was not disastrous. Slavery had profited individuals in the North, but in the Deep South it had reconfirmed itself as the cornerstone of an entire economy. Most Southern whites, moreover, could not tolerate the prospect of the huge free black population that would be created by emancipation programs which followed Northern examples.

Finally, it was the slaves themselves who made it so easy for elitist planters to espouse revolutionary republicanism. The disempowered blacks in the plantation South acted both as substitutes for and as a check on a restive white proletariat which might have otherwise applied revolutionary ideas about equality to a rebellion of its own against its slaveholding "betters." Throughout the antebellum period, lesser whites would continue to express racial solidarity with the planters, thereby muting social conflicts within the ruling race. In this significant sense, for Southern whites, the Revolution was profoundly pro-slavery. Outside of the middle ground, no manumission society existed anywhere in the South; no serious proposals for emancipation reached the legislature of any slave state. Thus, the Revolution endowed the planter elites and their slave-labor system with a powerful new legitimacy. But with legitimacy came new pangs of insecurity and a tough mood of sectional defensiveness. Slaveholders had now to accustom themselves to an emerging group of free states that ringed their borders. Moreover, antislavery-minded Yankees like Benezet continued to work with a rising generation of British reformers seeking to end slavery in the Caribbean islands, the American planters' southern flank. Most of all, slaveholders were aware that the Revolution had set many people, their own bondspeople included, to an unprecedented questioning of their way of life. Little wonder, then, that Southern leaders approached the deliberations of the 1787 Constitutional Convention with their slaveholding interests paramount.

Historians have sometimes asserted that the Founding Fathers betrayed the Revolution's commitment to emancipation by failing to incorporate national abolition into the Constitution. To be sure, the Philadelphia Convention contained many representatives identified with antislavery, and as the delegates met, abolitionist feeling in the North was also reaching its zenith. During this same year, the Continental Congress enacted the Northwest Ordinance, prohibiting slavery in territories north of the Ohio and east of the Mississippi rivers. Yet it is unlikely that the Founding Fathers could have placed Southern slavery on a course of extinction, even if they had wished to.

The makeup of the Convention guaranteed a direct potent voice to those determined to resist any infringements of the right to hold slaves. Slaveholding delegates constituted a powerful bloc in the Convention, capable of destroying the proceedings simply by walking out. To nationalist Founding Fathers, secession was to be avoided at all costs, regardless of one's dislike of slavery. The Founders firmly believed that the Revolution's goals were intimately linked with the sanctity of private property. Emancipation by federal coercion was thus as repugnant to them in theory as it was impossible in practice. Finally, by 1787, white Americans had come to sense the urgency of defining their newly won national citizenship, and one thing had become certain, regional differences and abolitionist sentiment notwithstanding: to claim genuine Americanness meant claiming to possess a white skin. It is not surprising, then, that the Founding Fathers incorporated protection for the planter classes into the Constitution rather than the liberation of their slaves.

The men who wrote the Constitution erected seemingly insuperable barriers against peaceful emancipation, though they did betray their squeamishness by avoiding the words "slave" and "slavery" in the document's language. Instead, they referred to "persons." The provision which permitted the outlawing of the African slave trade after 1808 reflected genuine antislavery feeling. But in many of its clauses the document clearly upheld the "peculiar institution." For instance, Article Four affirmed the right of masters to recover runaway slaves. But, most crucially, the Constitution granted the planter class exceptional leverage in national affairs. Article One provided that three-fifths of the slave population was to be counted for purposes of taxation and representation in the House of Representatives. In this way the Constitution guaranteed slaveholders political power which exceeded significantly their actual numbers. Their authority over their "chattel" drew reaffirmation from the supreme law of the land.

In succeeding years, abolitionists and politicians came to disagree strongly over the Founding Fathers' real attitudes toward slavery. Two points, however, seem beyond reasonable dispute.

First, the Constitution, while clearly sanctioning slaveowning, nevertheless contained so many sectional compromises as to appear highly ambiguous to later generations. Southern secessionists and Yankee unionists, not to mention quarreling factions of abolitionists, were to find historical justifications aplenty for irreconcilable points of view about the government's power over slavery. In short, the makers of the Constitution set no framework for future discussions of slavery. Without such a legacy, the disagreements were destined to become limitless.

A second point, less compelling in the long run perhaps, was nonetheless of much greater import to abolitionists of the eighteenth century. Whatever the Founders' private feelings about slavery, their primary concern lay in bringing stability out of the experience of revolution. The framers of the Constitution sought to guarantee the right of private property and to replace the tumults of localism with the majesty of national power. Theirs was a tough-minded stance, which subordinated disruptive innovations like abolition to the stern demands of national republicanism. So even as Northern legislatures continued to debate emancipation bills and black activists pressed their causes, the Philadelphia Convention announced a new era of national consolidation and conservatism. Nationhood achieved, the antislavery promise of the Revolution quickly dissipated.

To many African Americans, however, the Revolution's promises were hardly exhausted with the adoption of the Constitution. Politicized by the Revolution's struggles and empowered by increasing literacy, slaves and freedpeople now began collaborating extensively across regional boundaries. Throughout the North, from 1790 to 1820, legislative petitioning by African Americans was increasingly frequent, provoking objections from slaveholding politicians. In the South, mobile and literate slave artisans, boatmen, and dock workers absorbed and transmitted news from the wider world. During the 1790s, they described new outbreaks of revolution, first in France in 1789, then by 1792 in the Caribbean island of Santo Domingo, where tens of thousands of slaves and free blacks rose in bloody and ultimately successful revolt against their French overlords. Planters' anxieties deepened and African Americans' hopes grew as displaced slaveholders from Santo Domingo converged in large numbers on Virginia and the Carolinas, bringing their slaves with them. Fearing that the virus of black rebellion was spreading to their own mainland slaves, nervous planters restricted slave imports from the West Indies, increased surveillance, and began deporting free African Americans.

From the planters' perspective, these responses were well justified. Throughout the 1790s, networks of political communication between slaves, free blacks, and even poorer whites continued to expand within the slave states. African Americans worked to extend the "spirit of '76" as incidents of localized slave resistance multiplied along with emancipation petitions from literate blacks to federal and state governments. Late in 1800, these elements of dissent finally crystallized into serious rebellion: an attempt on the part of an emancipationist army of slave artisans led by Gabriel Prosser to capture Richmond, Virginia, kill its wealthiest residents, and spread rebellion throughout the South. Though Prosser's conspiracy was discovered before it could be carried out, evidence collected by frantic planters confirmed that the plot had been remarkably widespread, thanks to the involvement of black boatmen and artisans who traveled so extensively across the state. The slogan on the banner under which Gabriel's army proposed to march — DEATH OR LIBERTY — made clear the rebels' ideological indebtedness to the American Revolution. After more than thirty hangings, Virginia authorities finally declared the insurrection quelled. But the communication networks among slaves remained very much intact, and much on the minds of leading slaveholders. Little wonder, then, that few whites demurred in the 1790s when Congress, as authorized by the Constitution, enacted a fugitive-slave law, or when Kentucky and Tennessee were admitted as new slave states. By 1810, as Eli Whitney's cotton gin opened vast new opportunities for the planter class to adapt slave labor to a new and extraordinarily profitable commodity, militant abolitionism in white America had run its course.

As fear of black initiative grew among whites across the nation, many leading figures transferred their concerns about slavery to the American Colonization Society. Founded in 1816, the Colonization Society proposed to resettle American free blacks in Africa and encouraged voluntary emancipations. The Society attempted thus to offset the charge that emancipation would saddle the nation with an intolerably large, volatile free black population. The Society also suggested to Southern whites, now justifiably nervous about insurrection, that means were available for reducing the unenslaved black population. The idea of solving America's race problems by transporting its unwilling black inhabitants was wildly impractical, a financial and organizational impossibility. And those were not the only drawbacks. Some sensitive planters would oppose the idea as a subtle assault on the master-slave relationship. Most of all, black leaders spurned such colonization as a racist insult, a plan concocted by white supremacists to serve their own ends. "[We] prefer being colonized in the most remote corner of the land of our nativity, to being exiled to a foreign country," declared free African Americans from Richmond, Virginia, in 1817. When black leaders did endorse colonization, it was only because they feared that the bigotry of white America had left their race facing a future of unrelieved misery.

Despite these obstacles, colonization held a compelling attraction to those seeking moderate alternatives to wholesale emancipation, civil war, servile insurrection, and black equality. During the 1820s, the peak years of the American Colonization Society, eminent clerics and such nationally prominent slaveowning politicians as Henry Clay, James Monroe, and John Marshall endorsed the Society's efforts to establish a colony for transported blacks in Liberia. Clearly, these individuals could not be considered serious abolitionists. Yet, during these years, some colonizationists did believe that they were sponsoring Christian uplift of blacks while alleviating some of slavery's most objectionable features. Accordingly, they urged masters to educate their bondspeople for new lives as Christian missionaries after selective manumission and transferal to Liberia. By enlightening his slaves, the master, too, was to learn Christian benevolence, thereby lessening the brutalities of slaveownership. Many colonizationists expected that attachment to slavery would gradually diminish and that, perhaps, the institution itself would someday come to an end.

Here was a vision with considerable attraction for well-educated, idealistic young men anxious in the 1820s to forward the moral improvement of America's black population. Among them were an impressive number of individuals such as William Lloyd Garrison who were soon to be preeminent among militant abolitionists. For these white radicals-in-the-making, colonization functioned as a respectable outlet for misgivings about slavery in an era which demanded ideological conservatism. In this respect, the Society served as an important transition for abolitionists-to-be. Its publications acquainted them with the evils of slavery and the oppressed lot of America's free blacks. And later on, as young abolitionists renounced gradualism, the Society became a crucial focus of youthful rebellion against traditional solutions to the problem of slavery. The American Colonization Society thus foreshadowed radical abolitionism while at the same time affirming the status quo.

Although few Americans in the 1820s openly objected to

slavery, the issue did spark serious sectional conflict and racial discontent. From 1819 to 1821, politicians flirted with secession as Congress, over Northern protests, admitted Missouri into the Union as a slave state. Organized with a state constitution upholding slavery, Missouri applied for statehood in 1819. At once, New England politicians protested that America's republican future, which lay in its Western settlements, should not be jeopardized by any expansion of slave labor. Suddenly, Northern and Southern representatives found themselves in hostile opposition to one another; the issue of slavery's place in westward expansion awakened deeply conflicting visions of the Republic's development. Compromise finally soothed this crisis when Maine was admitted as a free state along with the slave state Missouri, while slavery was excluded from Louisiana Purchase lands north of 36° 30'.

Two years later, in 1821, in Charleston, South Carolina, local whites ruthlessly suppressed what they confirmed to have been a far-flung conspiracy led by freedman Denmark Vesey and supported by Charleston's black artisans as well as by ferry boatmen throughout the state's coastal parishes. As in Gabriel Prosser's earlier conspiracy, investigations documented the surprising extent of the slaves' networks of communication, which mass hangings and banishments presumably could not eliminate. Yet neither the Missouri controversy nor the Vesey conspiracy, each an undeniably serious crisis involving slavery, aroused fundamental misgivings among whites about the legitimacy of the institution. The best that Thomas Jefferson could offer was the anguished observation that "we are holding the wolf by the ears."

On a much deeper level, a complex set of forces was at work during the 1820s which soon led, among white New Englanders, to an abolitionist movement of unparalleled scope and intensity. Inspired by Christian egalitarianism and a profound sense of personal guilt, young men and women were soon to take up the immense task of convincing their countrymen that slavery was a terrible sin, and that race prejudice was at war with the teachings of Jesus. They would appeal to the precedents set by the Revolution and the Declaration of Independence. Their opponents pointed to the Constitution's "three-fifths clause" and applauded the Revolution's guarantee of private property. The values and precedents of the American Revolution, ambiguous in the extreme, would prove serviceable to all participants in these renewed debates over slavery — which ultimately led the nation to civil war.

2

IMMEDIATE EMANCIPATION

American society in the late 1820s presented well-informed white evangelicals with tremendous challenges. For the better part of a decade, Protestant moralists throughout the North had warned against the citizenry's all-absorbing interest in material wealth, self-indulgence, and party politics. Infidelity, they were told, flourished on the frontiers; vice reigned supreme in the burgeoning cities. In politics, God-fearing men were exhorted to combat the demagogues of Jacksonian Democracy, whose political party endorsed popular rule, divorced Christian morality from government, and harvested votes from rumbesotted day laborers and illiterate pioneers. For pious wives and mothers, the challenge was equally daunting. Only their innate female "purity," they were assured, protected the rising generation from an inundation of materialism, godlessness, and vice. Without the guidance of a redeeming female influence, men would fall prey to their basest instincts and the nation would abandon its Christian way of life. Exaggerated as such claims may seem, they were grounded in reality. Yankee Protestantism was indeed facing immense new challenges from a society in the throes of dramatic social change. As godly men and women struggled to discharge their Christian responsibilities, a volatile new crusade for immediate emancipation took form.

By the end of the 1820s, America was undergoing what historians refer to as the "market revolution." Powerful commercial networks had begun linking all sections of the country; canals, the telegraph, mass-circulation newspapers, and, soon, railroads reinforced this thrust toward regional interdependence. Rapidly expanding Northern businesses depended as never before on trade with the South. The cotton revolution which swept the Mississippi–Alabama–Georgia frontier stimulated textile manufacturing and shipping in the Northeast. In the Northwest, yet another economic boom took shape as businessmen and farmers in Ohio, Indiana, and Illinois developed lucrative relationships with the Eastern seaboard, and the populations of Northern cities grew apace, led by a rapidly expanding, wage-earning working class. Tough-minded politicians created party machines which catered to these new interests and to the "common man's" secular preferences.

These cosmopolitan forces of economic interdependence, urbanization, class differentiation, and democratic politics presented evangelicals with a painful contradiction: many of the pious moralists who so feared social disruption were actually strong promoters of the market revolution. As these Protestant bankers, manufacturers, and commercial traders pursued economic expansion and diversification throughout the North, they also struggled to infuse moral purpose into the disruptive commercial culture that accompanied their innovations.

They sought to combat popular excesses with their own democratic weapons. Throughout the 1820s, pious New Englanders mounted an impressive counterattack against the "immorality" that they had inadvertently helped to encourage by putting to new uses techniques they had perfected in their business affairs: the publicity campaign, fund-raising, and the

efficiently managed bureaucratic agency. With the hope of re-
vitalizing American religion and social relations, the American
Tract Society and the Temperance Union spewed forth
thousands of pamphlets which exhorted the unredeemed and
the inebriated to repent. Busy missionary societies sent witnesses to backcountry settlements, the waterfront haunts of
Boston's seamen, the bordellos of New York City. These agencies offered no criticism of the market revolution itself. Instead,
they envisioned a reassertion of traditional New England values on a scale equivalent to the transformation taking place
within the economy. At the same time, although unintentionally, these programs for Christian restoration stimulated in pious young men and women stirrings of more fundamental
revolt.

As in the decades before the American Revolution, social
discontent and political alienation once again found widespread
expression through massive spiritual awakenings; throughout
the 1820s, a series of Great Revivals heralded a Yankee Protestant resurgence. Like their eighteenth-century predecessors,
powerful evangelists such as Charles G. Finney and Lyman
Beecher urged people, even seemingly irredeemable sinners, to
strive for holiness and choose new lives of sanctification. As in
the 1750s, God was depicted as insisting that the saved perform
acts of benevolence, expand the boundaries of Christ's kingdom, and take on a personal responsibility to improve society.
Evangelicals by the thousands flocked to the Tract Society, the
Sunday School Union, the Ladies' Benevolent Associations, the
temperance and peace organizations, the manual-labor movement, and the Colonization Society. Seeking moral reformation, certainly not revolution, white evangelicals dreamed of a
glorious era of national reform: emancipated from liquor, prostitution, atheism, pauperism, and popular politics, the redeemed masses would gladly submit to the leadership of
Christian statesmen, not to the blandishments of that whiskey-

drinking gambler, duelist, bigamist, Indian-killer, and un-churched slaveowner, President Andrew Jackson. From this morally charged setting sprang New England's crusade against slavery. Radical reformers of all varieties, not just abolitionists, traced their activism to the revivals of the 1820s. The revivals of the Revolutionary era had aroused strong abolitionist tendencies but had not generated ongoing movements for radical change. The evangelical outbursts of the 1820s, by contrast, fostered sustained rebellion among thousands of young men and women. The result was a bewildering variety of reform movements, of which abolitionism, though extremely influential, was but one.

Several factors help to explain this. First, the revivalists of the 1820s found it impossible to isolate or attack a specific source for the immorality that so disturbed them. There was no tyrannical king or corrupt parliament to turn against, no glorious political brotherhood to join, such as the Sons of Liberty, no exalted goal to achieve, such as national independence. The evangelical crusaders of the 1820s had few points of reference on which to fix. Few institutions or popular leaders commanded their loyalties. Lacking these, revivalists sensed that infidelity and corruption crowded in from all quarters. Their own dedication was all that stood between a sinning nation and God's all-consuming retribution. Second, these new revivalists harbored unprecedented feelings of revulsion at the thought that people were physically abusing one another and subjecting one another to moral degradation. Seeing themselves as pathbreaking humanitarians, evangelical reformers had no tolerance for those who inflicted hardship on others, an attitude that prefigured not only abolitionism but also crusades against flogging, dueling, prostitution, and capital punishment. This, indeed, was a radical temperament, driven by guilt, which urged a lifetime of intense Christian struggle and a searching reexamination of long-accepted customs and institutions.

While the ethos of revivalism gave rise to anxiety, the network of benevolent agencies opened opportunities for young Americans unknown to their eighteenth-century counterparts. The missionary agencies and even the revivals themselves were organized along complex bureaucratic lines which created new careers of social activism for young men and women. Among men, earnest ministerial candidates began accepting full-time positions as circuit riders, regional agents, newspaper editors, and schoolteachers, with salaries underwritten by the benevolent agencies. One important abolitionist-to-be, Joshua Leavitt, spent his first years after seminary editing *The Seaman's Friend*, an evangelical periodical for sailors. Another, Elizur Wright, Jr., was employed by the American Tract Society. For pious women such as Lydia Maria Child and Abigail Kelly, revivalism opened opportunities to break through restrictions of family into charitable associations and prayer groups managed exclusively by people of their own gender.

Most important to abolitionism was the effect of revivalism on the ministry itself. Once open only to an elite, the ministry had by the 1820s become a common profession. Spurred by an expanding scope of national activity, seminaries increased their enrollments as they attracted young men eager to aid in America's regeneration. Included were some destined to number among abolitionism's dominant figures: Samuel J. May, Theodore D. Weld, and Joshua Leavitt, to name only a few. As these young clerics soon discovered, the composition of their congregations had also been transformed by revivalism, with energetic women now constituting a majority of members. Revivalism, from the first, gave strong impetus to women's activism, and young ministers had little choice but to take their female parishioners seriously. Given the unprecedented inten-

sity of commitment, it is not surprising that some of these enthusiasts began entertaining ideas that led to abolitionism.
There is persuasive evidence that family background and
upbringing predisposed certain young New Englanders to a
radical outlook. Many of abolitionism's prominent leaders were
raised by well-educated Presbyterians, Congregationalists,
Quakers, and Unitarians who participated extensively in revivalism and its benevolent projects. In such families, as numerous biographers have attested, a stern emphasis on moral
uprightness and social responsibility prevailed. Early in life,
these young men and women learned the importance of living
by their families' personal ethics rather than by the more per-
missive standards of the outside world. Parents inculcated a
high degree of religious and social conscience in their children.
In their reminiscences, abolitionists paid homage to strong-
minded mothers and fathers whose intense religious fervor
dominated the household. In his early years, Wendell Phillips
constantly turned to his mother for instruction, and after her
death he confessed that "whatever good is in me, she is responsible for." Thomas Wentworth Higginson, Arthur and
Lewis Tappan, and William Lloyd Garrison became, like Phillips, leading abolitionists and also internalized the religious dictates of dominating mothers. Sidney Howard Gay, Theodore
D. Weld, James G. Birney, Elizur Wright, Jr., and Elijah P.
Lovejoy are abolitionists who modeled their early lives to fit
the intentions of exacting fathers. Young women who entered
the movement usually sought the approbation of their fathers,
as in the cases of Elizabeth Cady Stanton and Maria Weston
Chapman.

Whichever parent became the child's example, the adults'
expectations seldom varied. Displays of conscience and upright
behavior brought the rewards of parental love and approval.
Children also learned that sexual self-control was a vital part
of righteous living. Parents stressed prayer and benevolent

deeds as substitutes for "carnal thoughts" and intimacy; they associated sexual sublimation with family stability and personal redemption. During his years at boarding school and later at Harvard, Wendell Phillips strove to satisfy his mother on all these counts. Lewis Tappan, too, remembered how hard he had worked "to be one of the best scholars, often a favorite with the masters, and a leader among the boys in our play." When he was twenty and living away from home, Tappan still received admonitions from his mother about the pitfalls of sex. Recalling a dream, she wrote: "Methought you had, by frequenting the theatre, been drawn into the society of lewd women, and had contracted a disease that was preying upon your constitution." For his part, Tappan had sworn to "enjoy a sound mind and body, untainted by vice." A strong sense of their individuality, a deadly earnestness about moral issues, confidence in their ability to master themselves and to improve the world—these were the qualities which so often marked leading abolitionists in their early years. Above all, these reformers believed in their own superiority and fully expected to become leaders.

Of course, not all children of morally assertive New Englanders became radical abolitionists. The sources of religious self-transformation are far too complex and personal to reduce to uniform family influences or social determinants. William Lloyd Garrison's brother, for example, despite his mother's tutelage, lapsed into alcoholism. Lewis Tappan's youngest brother, Benjamin, embraced atheism and followed the leadership of the very secular Andrew Jackson. But, in a general sense, the family-bred predisposition to pious self-criticism is hard to dismiss. Alienation and self-doubt ran especially deep among these sensitive young people.

Those who took up pastorates, seminary study, or positions in benevolent agencies were shocked to discover that the evangelical establishment was hardly free from the acquisitive taint and institutional inertia they had been taught to disdain. Expecting to lead communities of God-fearing families, young ministers like Theodore D. Weld confronted instead fragmented assemblies of undisciplined individuals and clerical superiors who acted much like bureaucrats. Weld wrote critically to the great evangelist Charles G. Finney that "revivals are fast becoming with you a sort of trade, to be worked at so many hours a day." Promoters of colonization, such as James G. Birney and Joshua Leavitt, became increasingly disturbed that many of their co-workers were far less interested in Christian benevolence than in ridding the nation of presumably "inferior" blacks. In politics, Lewis Tappan and William Lloyd Garrison searched desperately and without success for a truly Christian leader, an alternative to impious Andrew Jackson and the godless party he led.

Predictably, misgiving became ever more frequent among the young evangelicals as they began to question their abilities, to rethink their destinies, and to doubt the Christianity of the churches, seminaries, and benevolent societies. Just possibly, the nation was far more deeply mired in sin than anyone had imagined. Just possibly, parental formulas for godly reformation were fatally compromised. And, most disturbing of all, just possibly idealist-reformers themselves needed reforming — new relationships with God, new relationships with fellow human beings, and new visions of their deepest responsibilities as Christian Americans.

The powerful combination in the 1820s of Yankee conservatism, revivalist benevolence, New England upbringing, and social unrest was leading young evangelicals toward a radical religious vision, out of which a militant abolitionist movement began to take shape. Opposition to slavery certainly constituted a dramatic affirmation of one's pure Christian identity and commitment to a life of evangelical engagement. Economic exploitation, sexual license, physical abuse, gambling, drinking, and dueling, disregard for family ties — all traits associated with slaveowning — could easily be set in bold contrast with the pure ideals of Christian humanitarianism.

The few remaining whites whose abolitionism bespoke the legacies of the Revolution had little influence on these young New Englanders. The manumission societies first organized in the 1790s by Quakers and Moravian Brethren in Tennessee, Kentucky, and eastern North Carolina had all but collapsed by the end of the 1820s. By 1829, the middle ground's chief antislavery spokesman, Quaker editor Benjamin Lundy, had retreated northeastward from Tennessee to Baltimore and finally to Boston. The sudden emergence of immediate abolitionism in New England thus cannot be explained solely as a predictable offshoot of Yankee revivalism, a reflexive response to the disruptions of the market revolution, or a carryover from the Revolution's crusade. Far too many pious young New Englanders were exposed to all these influences yet showed no interest in abolition. When identifying the precipitating causes of the white abolitionist commitment, one must instead emphasize the interaction between the rebellious spiritual stirrings of these particular young New Englanders and the unprecedented slavery-related crises which opened the new decade.

In the early 1830s, well-organized African Americans suddenly began espousing violence in the cause of emancipation: slave uprising exploded in Virginia, and slaveholding extremists in South Carolina threatened to secede from the Union. In the Caribbean, this time in Jamaica, slaves rose again in mass rebellion and the British responded with an ambitious campaign of emancipation within their colonies. As youthful activists reacted to these rapidly multiplying conflicts, they found themselves launched headlong into abolitionism.

In this immediate historical context, two preeminent black activists — David Walker the militant pamphleteer and Nat Turner the slave insurrectionist — compelled white reformers to act. In this respect, black abolitionism was the parent of the white crusade. Walker, a former slave from North Carolina, was living in Boston in 1829 when he published his famous *Appeal.* A landmark in black political literature, Walker's *Appeal* condemned colonization as a white supremacist hoax, excoriated members of his own race for their passivity and ignorance, and called, as a last resort, for armed resistance. "I do declare," wrote Walker, "that one good black man can put to death six white men." Whites had never hesitated to kill blacks, he advised, so "if you commence . . . do not trifle, for they will not trifle with you." As Walker saw it, whites had betrayed the spirit of the American Revolution; African Americans alone understood the stark alternatives of "liberty or death."

Walker knew the communication networks that slaves and free blacks had been maintaining since Revolutionary days and he used them to distribute his pamphlet in the South. By 1830 and 1831, agitated slaveholders were discovering just how widely it was circulating in the South Carolina low country (the site of Denmark Vesey's earlier conspiracy), thanks to black seamen from Boston who took copies with them on voyages to Charleston. From there, literate slaves and free blacks passed on copies as far as New Orleans and Savannah. Some people were much relieved, therefore, when Walker was found dead in 1831 under mysterious circumstances in the doorway of his used-clothing store.

That same year, as if in response to Walker's writings, Southampton County, Virginia, erupted in the largest slave revolt in antebellum America. Only a week before, the Baptist exhorter Nat Turner had been secretly preaching and organizing as far away as the North Carolina border. As terrified white Virginians counted their dead (fifty-seven in all), few doubted that Turner in his frequent travels had attempted to coordinate his uprising in widely separate locations. No proof was ever found linking Turner's rebels with Walker's *Appeal,* but this was small solace to slaveholders. Soon after Nat Turner was tried and hanged, slave rebellion broke out in British Jamaica, another reminder to planters that slaves needed little outside influence to revolt.

The slaveholders' response to these racial crises was just as intense as the abolitionists'. In South Carolina, in 1831, planter politicians staged a confrontation with the federal government ostensibly over disagreements about national tariff policy. But beneath the Carolinians' demands that they be allowed either to nullify the tariff or to secede from the Union lay deep fears of rebellious slaves and meddling abolitionists, and the suspicion that the federal government might someday abolish slavery. Meantime, citizens in northern Virginia, the state's middle ground, began clamoring for gradual, compensated emancipation to avert future insurrections. At no other time before the onset of the Civil War would Southern political culture exhibit such instability.

As these frightening events unfolded, young evangelicals cast aside their self-doubt. Unfocused discontent gave way to soul-wrenching commitments to eradicating the sin of slavery. The combined actions of Nat Turner, the "Nullifiers," and David Walker confirmed with dramatic force that slavery was wholly responsible for society's degraded state. As Theodore D. Weld observed, the abolitionist cause "not only *overshadows* all others, but . . . absorbs them into itself. Revivals, moral Reform etc. will remain stationary until the temple is cleansed." The step-by-step solutions advocated by the abolitionists' reform-minded parents suddenly appeared to invite only God's retribution. Like William Lloyd Garrison, Arthur Tappan, and many others, James G. Birney sealed his commitment to immediate abolition by decrying colonization. The Colonization Society, Birney charged, acted as "an opiate to the consciences" of those who would otherwise "feel deeply and keenly the sin of slavery."

In one sense, the sudden espousal of immediate abolition can be understood as a strategic innovation developed to counter the failures of gradualism made manifest by Calhoun and the "Nullifiers." Slaveholders had certainly not been receptive to moderate emancipation. In England, too, where immediatism suddenly inspired an ambitious program of emancipation in the West Indies, the general public had remained unmoved by gradualist proposals. Demands for "immediate, unconditional, uncompensated emancipation" seemed perfect to young American idealists — the slogan, ringing with God's truth, was so free of moral qualifications that it inspired acts of self-liberation akin to the experience of religious conversion.

By freeing themselves from the shackles of gradualism, America's new generation of white abolitionists had finally triumphed over their feelings of selfishness, unworthiness, and alienation. Now they felt morally fit to take God's side in the struggle against the worldliness, license, and cruelty that slave-owning had come to embody. Spiritually transformed, immediatists now sensed themselves involved in a cosmic drama, a righteous war to redeem a fallen nation. They were now ready to make supreme sacrifices and prove their fitness in their new religion of antislavery. "Never were men called on to die in a holier cause," wrote Amos A. Phelps in 1835 as he began his first tour as an abolitionist lecturer. It was far better, he thought, to die "as the negro's plighted friend" than to "sit in silken security, the consentor to & abettor of the manstealer's sin."

The campaign for Protestant reassertion had brought forth a vibrant romantic radicalism. Orthodox evangelicals quite rightly recoiled in fear. Abolitionists now put their faith entirely in the individual's ability to recognize and redeem himself or herself from sin. No stifling traditions, no restrictive loyalties to institutions, no timorous concern for moderation or self-interest should be allowed to inhibit the free rein of Christian conscience. In its fullest sense, the phrase "immediate emancipation" described a transformed state of mind dominated by God and wholly at war with slavery. "The doctrine," wrote Elizur Wright, Jr., in 1833, "may be thus briefly stated":

> It is the duty of the holders of slaves to restore them to their liberty, and to extend to them the full protection of the law . . . to restore to them the profits of their labors. Also it is the *duty* of all men to proclaim this doctrine, to urge upon slaveholders *immediate emancipation*, so long as there is a slave — to agitate the consciences of tyrants, so long as there is a tyrant on the globe.

Embedded in this statement was a vision of a new America, a daring affirmation that people of both races could reestablish their relationships on the basis of justice and Christian fellowship. Like many other Americans who took up the burdens of reform, abolitionists envisioned their particular cause as leading to a society reborn in Christian harmony. Emancipation, like temperance, women's rights, and communitarianism, became synonymous with the redemption of humanity and the opening of a purer phase of history.

Abolitionists explained that they were not expecting some sudden Day of Jubilee when, with a shudder of collective remorse, the entire planter class would strike the shackles from all two million slaves and beg their forgiveness. Emancipation would be achieved gradually; but it must be immediately begun. Immediatists were also forced to rebut the recurring charge that their demands promoted emancipation by rebellion on the plantations. "Our objects are to save life, not destroy it," William Lloyd Garrison exclaimed in 1831. "Make the slave free and every inducement to revolt is taken away."

Few Americans believed these claims. Most thought that immediate emancipation would create a large, mobile, free population of inferior blacks. Most Northerners were content to discriminate harshly against their black neighbors while the slaves remained at a safe distance on faraway plantations. White supremacy and support for slavery were thus inextricably bound up with all phases of American political, economic, and religious life. Immediatist agitation was bound to provoke hostility from nearly every part of the social order, from the national religious denominations to the influential commercial interests that traded so lucratively between North and South.

By far the most consistent opponents of the abolitionist crusade were found in politics, which young reformers had long condemned as demagogic, secular, and captive of slaveholding interests. Jackson's Democratic Party was deliberately designed to uphold slavery in the South and white supremacy across the nation by catering particularly to the prejudices of urban workers, planters, proponents of forcible Indian removal, and anyone who set a high value on maintaining his sense of "whiteness." In the North, men who aspired to careers in Democratic Party politics had to obtain the approval of slaveholding party chiefs like John C. Calhoun, and Jackson himself. When anti-Jacksonian dissidents finally coalesced into the Whig Party in the 1830s, they relied on similar formulas for getting votes and recruiting leaders. Neither party dared to alienate pro-slavery interests in the South or racist supporters in the North. Moreover, as the Missouri controversy of 1820–21 had shown, political debates about slavery's extension westward caused party divisions along sectional lines. Party loyalty meant the suppression of all criticism of slavery.

In so hostile a political climate, immediatist goals were anything but limited. So was their capacity for disruption, for the abolitionists proposed to turn hundreds of millions of dollars' worth of slaves into millions of black citizens, eradicating two centuries of American racism. Yet they sincerely believed that they were promoting a conservative enterprise, and in certain respects this was an understandable (if misleading) self-assessment. Their unqualified attacks on slavery were, as they understood them, simply extensions of well-established evangelical methods. The Temperance Society's assault on liquor and the revivalist's denunciation of unbelief, though always pacifistic, was hardly characterized by rhetorical restraint. Besides, immediatists were not advocating bloody revolution. They relied solely on voluntary conversion. They defined their task as restoring time-honored American freedoms sanctioned by the American Revolution's founding ideals of freedom and equality to an unjustly deprived people. Except for their opposition to racism, they offered no criticism of ordinary Protestant values. Was it anarchy, they wondered, to urge that pure Christian morality replace what they imagined was the planter's sexual exploitation of his helpless female slaves? "Are we then fanatics," Garrison asked, "because we cry, Do not rob! Do not murder!?"

In their own eyes, then, newly emerging white abolitionists were behaving like patriots and peacemakers, not like incendiaries, as they opened their crusade. In slaveholding they had discovered the ultimate source of the moral collapse which so deeply disturbed them. The violence of Nat Turner and the secession threats of Calhoun's "Nullifiers" constituted evidence aplenty that the nation had jettisoned its republican values and Christian morals. Immediate abolition seemed to hold the promise of Christian reconciliation between races, sections, social classes, and individuals. All motive for race revolt, all reason for political strife, and all inducement for moral degeneracy would be swept away. Silence only invited the further spread of anarchy in a nation which Garrison described in 1831 as already "full of the blood of innocent men, women and babies — full of adultery and concupiscence — full of blasphemy, darkness and woeful rebellion against God — full of wounds and bruises and putrefying sores." Abolitionists were thus filled "with burning earnestness" when they insisted, as Elizur Wright, Jr., did, that "the instant abolition of the whole slave system is safe." Most other Americans remained firm in their beliefs to the contrary.

The abolitionists launched their crusade on a note of glowing optimism. Armed with moral certitude, they were also politically naïve. "The whole system of slavery will fall to pieces with a rapidity which will astonish," wrote Samuel E. Sewall, one of the first adherents of immediatism. Weld predicted in 1834 that complete equality for all blacks in the upper South was but two years away, and that "scores of clergymen in the slaveholding states . . . *are really with us.*" Anxious for the millennium, abolitionists wholly misjudged the depth of Northern racism, not to mention the receptivity of Southern whites.

All the same, there was power in the naïveté. Without this romantic faith that God would put all things right, abolitionists would have lacked the incentive and creative stamina for sustained assaults on slavery. By stressing spiritual intuition as a guide to reality, abolitionists succeeded in an unprecedented attempt to establish empathy with the slaves, vividly imagining what it was like to be stripped of one's autonomy, prevented from protecting one's family, and deprived of legal safeguards and the rewards of one's labor. To give slaves better food, fewer whippings, and some education was not enough. They deserved immediate justice, not charity. So convinced, and certain of ultimate victory, youthful holy warriors set out to persuade each American citizen to repent the sin of slavery.

3

MORAL SUASION

In December 1833, sixty-two abolitionists gathered in Philadelphia to form the American Anti-Slavery Society, a national organization devoted exclusively to promoting immediate emancipation. The meeting was well timed. Just six months earlier, in response to immediatist pressure in England, the British Parliament had enacted bills of emancipation for all slaves in the West Indies, an example which inspired Northern humanitarians to emulate it. Moreover, British reformers were once again involving themselves heavily in the American cause, a fact that American abolitionists welcomed, though in the eyes of opponents it tainted the movement as the plaything of foreign influence.

Most of all, the assembly represented an instructive cross section of those who were to lead the abolitionist crusade during the next three decades. Wealthy Lewis Tappan, for instance, spoke for socially respectable, wholly committed New York evangelicals, including his brother Arthur and editor Joshua Leavitt. James G. Birney, Elizur Wright, Jr., Theodore D. Weld, and other evangelicals based in northeastern Ohio and upstate New York also identified strongly with the Tappans. William Lloyd Garrison headed a heterogeneous delegation of New England Congregationalists like Samuel E. Sewall, Unitarians like Samuel J. May, and Quakers like John Greenleaf Whittier. Quakers accounted for twenty-one of the sixty-two in attendance. Four Quaker women, Lucretia Mott, Lydia White, Ester Moore, and Sara Pugh, as well as three black men, Robert Purvis, James McCrummell, and James G. Barbadoes, also signed the Society's Declaration of Sentiments.

Racially mixed and eager to attract the assistance of women, the American Anti-Slavery Society was controlled at its inception by talented and aggressive white men who combined religious zeal with aspirations as editors, businessmen, clerics, and philanthropists. The presence of only three African American delegates out of a total of sixty-two foreshadowed the struggles that lay ahead for black abolitionists in a predominantly white movement. And when the Quaker women excused themselves just before the male-only voting began, they, too, anticipated the future. A few days later, they convened to form their own Philadelphia Female Anti-Slavery Society, a clear harbinger of the close relationship that soon would develop between immediatism and women's rights.

For the moment, Garrison dominated the proceedings. Since January 1831, his Boston newspaper, *The Liberator*, had been gaining attention for its resounding attacks on colonization, its advocacy of immediate, uncompensated emancipation, and its willingness to open its columns to African Americans. Garrison's support among black community leaders across the Northeast had been growing since 1829, when he first denounced gradualism in speeches and editorials in various reform newspapers. That year, in Boston, David Walker named his newborn son Edward Garrison Walker in honor of the fiery young editor, and by 1833 African Americans made up more than sixty percent of the *Liberator*'s subscription list. Already famous for his harsh rhetoric, it was Garrison who wrote the American Anti-Slavery Society's Declaration of Sentiments.

In demanding immediate emancipation, Garrison's document explicitly endorsed non-violence and firmly rejected "the use of all carnal weapons" by abolitionists and slaves; Christian principle forbade "the doing of evil that good may come." Drawing ideologically on the precedents of the American Revolution, the Declaration noted that the colonists had "spilled human blood like water" while securing their own freedom, yet the patriots' grievances were "trifling" in comparison to those of the slave: "Our fathers were never slaves—never bought and sold like cattle—never shut out from the light of knowledge and religion—never subjected to the lash of brutal taskmasters." For citizens who enjoyed America's unique civil and religious liberty, toleration of slavery amounted to a personal sin "unequalled by any other on the face of the earth," and a "desecration" of the legacy of their "patriotic forbearers." Abolitionists, as patriots, were obliged to declare their unshakable opposition to colonization, to compensated emancipation, and to all laws upholding slavery. The slaves had every moral right to instant freedom and to the equal protection of the law; the bondspeople, not the slaveholders, deserved compensation. Every slaveowner was proven by Scripture to be a "MAN-STEALER," for he had dared to "usurp the prerogative of Jehovah" by violating another's inalienable rights.

Finally, in what was clearly the most difficult portion of the Declaration to live up to, the signers pledged to oppose all racial prejudice wherever it appeared. Abolitionists must, as Garrison put it, "secure to the colored population . . . all the rights and privileges that belong to them as men and as Americans . . . The paths of preferment, of wealth, and of intelligence should be opened as widely to them as to persons of white complexion."

The Declaration appeared to most Americans as undiluted fanaticism. Yet the signers were pledging themselves to goals which sharply magnified the era's dominant trends. In asserting that every person, regardless of race, should be "secure in his right to his own body—to the products of his own labor—to the protections of the law—to the common advantages of society," the Declaration claimed for African Americans those social and economic values which white men were eager to claim for themselves. Indeed, the call for immediate emancipation reflected a fervent desire to extend the tenets of economic self-reliance which were propelling the market revolution in the North.

Like the Democratic Party, their most fervent opponents in politics, abolitionists espoused the superiority of "free labor." Garrisonians no less than Jacksonians viewed with distrust any restriction on a man's freedom to contract for wages with potential employers and any "artificial" impediment preventing him from raising himself out of poverty. Although disagreeing deeply over which races should be included, the two groups concurred that every man had the inalienable right to advance by his own efforts. In this sense, the Declaration of Sentiments reflected the same spirit which inspired Jacksonian assaults on "artificial" monopolies, the anti-Masons' call for the abolition of secret social clubs, and the nativists' warnings about the Catholic hierarchy's "unnatural influence." Likewise, the Declaration documented the transformation occurring in the Northern labor force, where restrictive systems of artisanship and apprenticeship were rapidly being replaced by an ever-expanding class of independently contracting wage workers.

But here the similarities ended. Members of the American Anti-Slavery Society could hardly condone the Jacksonians' racism, their support of the workingman's right to carouse and sleep through church, or their easy assumption that slaves were simply property. As they dismantled the National Bank, lowered tariffs, and opened frontier lands to rapid settlement, Jacksonian Democrats explained that they were expanding the economic freedom of working people; citizens could now contract more widely for their labor, rise more rapidly in society, and invest as they wished — in a slave plantation or a free-labor enterprise, it made no difference. To the abolitionists, of course, it made all the difference in the world. Immediatism therefore contained a vision of a competitive system unparalleled in its inclusive belief that capitalism nurtured harmony among races and classes, as well as unlimited possibilities for upward social mobility. After emancipation, white abolitionists imagined, vocational independence, biblical morality, family autonomy, unimpeded mobility, and republican governance would rule in all parts of the nation. Slaves, their former masters, and liberated poor whites would all exercise their God-given rights to improve themselves, unhampered by race exploitation. The planters' sterile fields, producing now "but half a crop," would soon "smile beneath the plow of the freeman, the genial influence of just and equitable wages," as Elizur Wright, Jr., put it. The Mason–Dixon Line and the segregated school would give way to a homogeneous America in which, as Garrison wrote in 1831, "black skin will not be merely endurable, but popular." With an unprecedented demand for the liberation of black labor, the trumpet call of "immediate emancipation" foretold the eventual emergence of America's industrial economy. In a most fundamental sense, abolitionists were what they saw themselves to be — the prophets of a new age. Neither they nor most Jacksonians could have foreseen at such an early juncture that free-labor capitalism would eventually generate more class conflict than harmony and more exploitation than opportunity.

In Philadelphia, the delegates performed their prophetic roles with great seriousness. Members of the American Anti-Slavery Society pledged to begin organizing antislavery societies in every city, town, and village. Abolitionists would circulate antislavery tracts and newspapers, aiming to convert ministers and editors, men with direct influence over public opinion. In particular, abolitionists hoped to purify the churches. If clergymen endorsed immediatism and preached from Southern pulpits the sin of slaveholding, planters would be moved, for the sake of their souls, to release their bondspeople. The slaveholder, the race-hater, and the apathetic citizen were certain to repent, just as each abolitionist had repented all sinful complicity with oppression. The "dam of prejudice" would give way, unleashing "one still, deep, rapid, mighty current" of conversion, contrition, and emancipation. "Oh," rhapsodized Elizur Wright, Jr., in 1833, "how it will sweep away those refuges of lies!" Prejudice and slaveowning, outward manifestations of unrepentant hearts, were to be conquered with the tools of revivalism: "moral suasion," as immediatists referred to it. This is what the Declaration meant when it dedicated the American Anti-Slavery Society to "the destruction of error by the potency of truth—the overthrow of prejudice by the power of love—and the abolition of slavery by the spirit of repentance."

Having made these commitments, abolitionists of both races turned on the American Colonization Society, realizing from the outset that, to be effective, their demand for immediate emancipation had to be free of equivocation. From the first, they resisted all challenges from colonizationists to put forward "practical" schemes for easing the slaves' transition to freedom. "Practicality" implied compromise, and abolitionists rejected it utterly, since all such discussion deflected attention from society's fundamental problems—white racism and black enslavement. Until whites accepted African Americans as equals, digressions on incremental alternatives to immediatism would only reinforce prejudice and encourage complacency. This was what Garrison meant by his comment that "the genius of the abolition movement is to have *no plan.*"

In April 1831, an editorial by Garrison in *The Liberator* boldly proclaimed that the Colonization Society constituted a *"con-*

spiracy against human rights" which had to be crushed if the nation was to purge itself. Subsequent editions featured anti-colonization articles by black editorialists from every part of New England, a clear indication of African Americans' deep interest in the burgeoning white crusade. After the founding of the New England Anti-Slavery Society in 1832, abolitionist agents began organizing anticolonization rallies in Massachusetts, Connecticut, Vermont, and New Hampshire, and Garrison conducted a series of similar meetings with African American congregations in Massachusetts, Connecticut, and New York. That same year, with funding supplied by Arthur Tappan, Garrison published his *Thoughts on African Colonization*, an unwieldy compendium made up, in part, of racist quotations from leading colonizationists. Garrison also included extended statements from black spokesmen which demonstrated their unremitting hostility to emigration.

For the young white abolitionists, these were exhilarating, fulfilling times. As they battled the colonizationists and initiated their first moral-suasion projects, they felt themselves bound together in a holy association of selfless and kindred spirits. Fifty years afterward, Lydia Maria Child recalled with nostalgia that "mortals were never more sublimely forgetful of self" than were the antislavery men and women of the 1830s. "How quick the 'mingled flute and trumpet eloquence' of [Wendell] Phillips responded to the clarion-call of Garrison . . . How wealth poured in from the ever open hands of Arthur Tappan, Gerrit Smith, and thousands of others." Such feelings seemed almost sufficient recompense for pleading the slaves' cause. Certainly, the spirit of brotherhood and sisterhood which suffused the abolitionists' letters to one another suggested that these reformers drew satisfying contrasts between their circles of holiness and love and the pretense and racism of the "unredeemed" world. These spiritually restless young men and women had now invented a religion of their own, a sanctified community which filled the enormous void created when they had rejected orthodox revivalism and which would sustain them during the struggles that lay ahead.

The inspiration of immediatism radiated in other directions as well. White women in many parts of the North quickly responded to the challenge of moral suasion, just as the Philadelphia Quaker women had done. Soon they began to found their own separate antislavery societies designed to bring the message to "the rising generation" while inviting their "colored sisters" to join them. The Female Anti-Slavery Societies that suddenly came to life in Boston, Philadelphia, Rochester, and New York City mirrored similar organizations of women that began springing up throughout the Northeast. The boundaries of the "separate sphere" were now extending far beyond the household. When men in Philadelphia laughingly shouted "Go home and spin!" at women who had assembled to take up abolitionist work, their dismissive comment registered a serious concern that immediatism was undermining long-established male prerogatives.

Though African Americans constituted but a small and symbolic presence in these new antislavery societies, black communities across the North responded broadly to the white immediatists' call. When the American Anti-Slavery Society appealed for auxiliary branches to be organized throughout the nation, groups organized exclusively by blacks quickly became active in remote hamlets such as Troy, Michigan, and Mount Pleasant, Ohio, as well as in major cities like Rochester, Newark, Philadelphia, and New York. In Boston, the Juvenile Garrison Independent Society demonstrated just how subversive of prevailing custom immediatism could be when it enrolled together young African Americans of both genders between the ages of ten and twenty. Prominent African American leaders such as James Forten in Philadelphia and Nathaniel Paul in New York City began making important new connections within networks of Yankee reform, and with one another. The spirit of community building that had surfaced so powerfully among Northern black city dwellers in the 1780s and 1790s was now renewing itself, this time with a more pronounced insurgent spirit.

The emerging elements of black and white activism came together most dramatically in 1834, when a famous student rebellion at Cincinnati's Lane Seminary led to the founding of Oberlin College. The struggle began when Arthur Tappan, the wealthiest of the abolitionists, decided to turn the seminary into a citadel of immediatism. Tappan had already contributed heavily to Lane's endowment and had hired its president, the acclaimed evangelical preacher Lyman Beecher, when he decided to send a powerful abolitionist emissary to the seminary. The charismatic Theodore D. Weld brought with him young friends like Henry B. Stanton who, like him, were well schooled in the formulas of immediatism and who were attracted by an admissions policy that encouraged "people of color" to apply. After Weld's arrival, and after more than two weeks of prayerful "protracted sessions," the Lane students and faculty endorsed immediatism, organized an antislavery society, and began developing reform projects in the local African American community. A few students even suspended their studies for a year for full-time service in a black elementary school.

Cincinnati's white citizens, some of whom had only four years earlier rioted viciously against their black neighbors, threatened retaliation. The worried trustees ordered students and faculty to disband their antislavery society, and President Beecher could effect no compromise. Forty students led by Weld thereupon renounced their affiliation with the seminary and pursued their activities in Cincinnati with even greater zeal before finally withdrawing to a more welcoming location in Oberlin, a small town in northern Ohio. Once again, the Tappans supplied funding for a new college, and for the first time in the history of higher education, at Oberlin, instruction was open equally to men and women regardless of race. Weld declined a professorship, preferring to evangelize the countryside against slavery. Still, he retained close ties with Oberlin, which soon became the hub of Western abolitionism and the nation's first example of integrated coeducational learning. As the college prospered, it demonstrated the magnetic power of immediatism to draw people together across lines of gender and race.

By projecting its influence into the middle ground, immediatism even blurred boundaries between North and South. To abolitionists, the repentant slaveholder was a most valuable source of testimony, and Southern-born crusaders such as Marius Robinson, James T. Allen, and James G. Birney bore authentic witness to slavery's evils. These adherents also heightened the abolitionists' initial expectation that Southern whites could actually be won over. "I read with tears of joy and gratitude!" exclaimed Lewis Tappan in 1835 after learning of Birney's conversion.

But the Southern immediatists were not harbingers of more general repentance. Although from slaveholding families, Southerners like Birney, Angelina Grimké (who later married Theodore D. Weld), and her sister Sarah all had had an upbringing which departed significantly from plantation norms. Birney's Presbyterian father, for example, was the most prestigious slaveowner in Danville, Kentucky, where he took the lead in evangelical projects that neighbors whispered were dangerously close to New England ways. While promoting a decidedly antislavery form of colonization and supporting temperance, the elder Birney had also insisted on a sound Yankee education at Princeton for his son. Such an exceptional background set young James Birney on a course which began with colonization and ended with uncompromising immediatism.

Although Birney and the Grimké sisters remained exceptions, Yankee abolitionism did exert an enduring influence within the upper South. In long-settled border areas of Virginia and Maryland and in more recently developed parts of eastern Tennessee, central and northern Kentucky, and northern Missouri, the free-labor culture of the middle ground continued to solidify. Here Quakers, Moravians, and free-will Baptists exhibited a preference for commercial careers, evangelicalism, and benevolent activity. In places like Jonesboro, Tennessee, Guilford, North Carolina, and Baltimore County, Maryland, pious citizens mingled with free blacks, observed temperance vows, supported missionaries, endorsed humanitarian projects, and sometimes became involved with Northern immediatists.

For their part, immediatists were aware that slavery remained a debatable subject within the upper South. Early in their careers, prominent leaders such as Lucretia Mott, William Lloyd Garrison, Theodore D. Weld, and Gamaliel Bailey traveled extensively in the region, stimulating antislavery feelings and deepening their own hostility to slaveowning by confronting the practice directly. Less famous antislavery missionaries Thomas Garrett, Daniel Worth, and Adam Crooks spent their lives quietly preaching emancipation and aiding fugitives. Charles T. Torrey, Daniel Drayton, and Calvin Fairbank, by contrast, achieved national prominence when jailed by Southern authorities for attempting to rescue slaves. Throughout the antebellum decades, Northern abolitionists were able to array themselves directly against slaveholding from within the South.

In the upper South, indigenous dissenters also began to establish themselves. In Louisville, Kentucky, Cassius Clay began his rise to national prominence in the later 1830s by publishing an antislavery newspaper, while in nearby Berea, John Fee established an enduring abolitionist enclave that ultimately nurtured Berea College, the South's first racially integrated institution of higher learning. In Baltimore, Quaker patriarch Edward Tyson openly assisted fugitives, underwrote

African American education, and subscribed to an antislavery newspaper published by his neighbor, James Snodgrass. But the most telling expression of middle-ground antislavery was the fearful response of whites in northern Virginia to Nat Turner's insurrection, to Walker's *Appeal*, and to the rapidly mounting evidence of activism among Southern blacks. In 1831 and 1832, upcountry representatives to the Virginia legislature forced a fateful debate on a gradual-emancipation bill which mandated compensation for masters and expulsion for freed blacks. Though the measure was decisively defeated, its lesson to Deep South planters was clear: the border areas were not to be trusted as a first line of defense against antislavery. Farther south, however, whites of all classes closed ranks, thereby ending most of the collaboration by common people of both races first begun in the seventeenth century.

Because of his slaveholding background, James Birney understood Southern white suspicions well when he warned his fellow abolitionists in 1835 that the "slaveholder's tenacity" made him "perfectly at ease in his iniquity." The prospects of converting him were indeed small, and "repentance is far off." As Birney offered this prediction, many Southern whites were busily confirming its accuracy. Spurred by the crises of 1831 and by the initial publication of Garrison's *Liberator*, town meetings throughout the Deep South put up rewards for the apprehension of persons circulating abolitionist literature. In South Carolina, Governor James Hamilton, Jr., and Senator Robert Y. Hayne attempted to enlist the Mayor of Boston in efforts to silence Garrison; Georgia's legislature appropriated five thousand dollars to reward the daring soul who would seize the Boston editor and bring him south for trial.

In retrospect, this deep-seated hostility is hardly surprising. Even before the rise of immediatism, some planters had concluded that serious discussions of slavery were too subversive to be permitted and had developed aggressive justifications of the institution as a beneficial social force. Following the terrifying events of 1831, many Southern whites became all the more wedded to their "peculiar institution" and sensitive to the dangers of agitation. With the defeat of the Virginia emancipation bill, forthright opposition to slavery in Southern politics ended. So did any chance of abolitionist negotiation with moderate slaveholders, if, indeed, such a group had ever existed. Henceforth, criticism by "outsiders" would not be tolerated. Hostility to immediatism from Northern white society was equally predictable. Because so many national institutions had come to rely on slaveholders' support, Northern politicians, ministers, and businessmen had practical reasons aplenty for suppressing the abolitionists. Beneath these hardheaded motives lay powerful racial prejudices that permeated Northern society ever more deeply as the market revolution continued its course. As young Frederick Douglass put it vividly in his first speech as an abolitionist: "Prejudice against color is stronger north than south; it hangs around my neck like a heavy weight. It presses me out from my fellow men . . . I have met it every step the three years I have been out of slavery."

In an increasingly competitive economy, a "white" skin had compelling political meaning, especially among immigrants who entered Northern cities as unskilled or semiskilled laborers. To suddenly learn that one's "whiteness" guaranteed social privileges and political equality constituted an essential part of immigrant acculturation and created a militantly racist solidarity with native-born whites. By the later 1830s, workingmen at first sympathetic to abolitionism because of their opposition to both "chattel slavery" and "wage slavery" had begun to change their minds. As the social gulf widened between wage earners and employers, intensifying racism muted a similar growing potential for class conflict; in an ever-tightening labor market, the unskilled Boston dock worker was always quick to repulse any challenge to his sense of fraternal "whiteness" with the Winthrops and the Adamses. Upper-class whites, for their part, were as eager to suppress the abolitionists as were their employees, since moral suasion repudiated their leadership not only as colonizationists but also in the churches and benevolent societies over which they presided so proudly. The forces compelling this alliance of whites across the widening gap of economic inequality were powerful indeed.

From its inception, the immediatist crusade leveled wholesale assaults on this inter-class compound of prejudice and self-interest. Moral suasion would never triumph, abolitionists correctly reasoned, if "negrophobic" attitudes prevented the unconverted from joining their crusade. Seeking to dissipate racism, white abolitionists quoted the Bible to emphasize that God had made all men in His image. Appealing to history, they pointed to figures like Hannibal, Alexandre Dumas, Crispus Attucks, Saint Augustine, the Egyptian Pharaohs, and others with reputedly dark skin. In fugitive slaves like Frederick Douglass and in freeborn blacks like Samuel Ringgold Ward, white abolitionists found African Americans with superior intellectual skills and public demeanor that wholly belied the myth of innate inferiority. The oppressive environment created by slavery and discrimination, abolitionists argued, produced the economic backwardness, intellectual dullness, and moral insensibility which whites so insistently claimed were the hallmarks of African American culture. As Lydia Maria Child once asserted, "In the United States, colored persons have scarcely any chance to rise. But if colored people are well treated, and have the same inducements to industry as others, they [will] work as well and behave as well." So convinced, white reformers set about encouraging local self-help among Northern free blacks. As they did so, they ignited a firestorm of reprisal, as Prudence Crandall, an abolitionist schoolteacher, quickly discovered.

In 1833 Prudence Crandall, a Quaker schoolmistress, decided to admit a black child to her private academy for girls in Canterbury, Connecticut. After incensed white parents had withdrawn their children, Crandall, at Garrison's suggestion, began to recruit an all-black student body. The townspeople then placed the school under an economic boycott, poisoned Crandall's well with animal feces, and lobbied successfully for a state law which made operating such a school illegal. Crandall defied the law, and spent a number of months in jail. Upon her release in 1834, she announced that classes would resume, whereupon Canterbury's citizens assembled, attacked the building with crowbars, and tried to set it on fire. The school never reopened, though in 1838 the Connecticut legislature repealed the law which had thwarted Crandall's experiment. This failure, disheartening as it was, only foreshadowed the harrowing mob violence which awaited the young immediatists.

From the late 1820s to the late 1830s, Americans witnessed civil violence unparalleled in their national history. Rioting had become a widely accepted method of addressing society's burgeoning religious, ethnic, political, and class tensions as mobs and lynchings erupted everywhere — in cities, in the countryside, in the North as well as in the South. By 1834, angry citizens had attacked Catholic convents in upstate New York, looted the homes of Baltimore bankers, torched the dwellings of blacks in Philadelphia and Boston, and disrupted a number of Masonic Lodge meetings. So commonplace had violence become that, especially after 1834, there was in some quarters a fear of total social disintegration. In 1834, abolitionists discovered that they, too, were targets of mob action, for Jacksonian society invited vigilantism. In a political culture that emphasized the individual citizen's primacy, white men responded even with violence to the imperative to participate directly and instinctively in the shaping of public life. President Andrew Jackson certainly reinforced such feelings when he claimed that he served democracy best when he took the law unto himself in annihilating Indians, abolishing banks, and defying the courts.

Many white Americans came to believe that legal procedures were hopeless tangles of tradition which only impeded true democracy and which the unscrupulous manipulated for their own ends. Mobs, it was argued, preserved popular rule by stopping such insidious groups when duly appointed authorities appeared hamstrung by legal formalities. By their own estimate, rioters were never disturbers of the peace, only restorers of social order. Yet mob action against the abolitionists did not begin until the abolitionists themselves had set the scene by creating a widespread, well-funded movement. When Garrison first began distributing *The Liberator* in 1831, his denunciations incited no local violence. But two years later, on October 2, 1833, fifteen hundred New Yorkers stormed the Chatham Chapel looking for Garrison and Arthur Tappan. The Chatham Chapel incident illustrates how abolitionist successes inspired mob violence.

During the two-year interval between 1831 and 1833, abolitionists could cite major accomplishments. January 1832 had witnessed the formation of the New England Anti-Slavery Society and the start of campaigns to aid free blacks and to discredit the American Colonization Society. By late 1833, abolitionist organizations had expanded from four local societies in two states to forty-seven in ten states. In far-off Hudson, Ohio, Elizur Wright, Jr. was quoting Garrison's *Thoughts* in debates at Colonization Society meetings; in still farther-off London, Garrison himself had captured the cash subsidies of English abolitionists, much to the colonizationists' dismay. Back in New York, in this same year, Arthur Tappan stunned colonizationists further by throwing his immense wealth behind Garrison. With contributions to their cause plummeting, the colonizationists suddenly sensed themselves under siege by a

far-flung network of Anglo-American enemies. Inspired by colonizationists' warnings of racial "amalgamation" and fearing
unspeakable transformations of their own social order, members of New York City's white working class began to assemble in October 1833.

Members of anti-abolitionist mobs, rich as well as poor, believed with good reason that the "friends of the slave" were
shredding the social fabric. Wealthy anti-abolitionists represented for the most part the North's older provincial elites,
prominent lawyers, doctors, judges, and congressmen, high-
ranking professionals and men involved in local business.
Abolitionists referred to them with disdainful accuracy as "gentlemen of property and standing." In an age of growing com-
mercialization and regional interdependence, such individuals
depended for their livelihood on local economies which were
being eroded by the market revolution. Their status also depended on their leadership in hierarchical organizations such
as the Episcopal Church, the "old school" (anti-evangelical)
Presbyterian Church, and the local Colonization Society. Many
anti-abolitionists also had strong roots in local political juntos,
regarding themselves as "zealous" Whigs or Democrats.

Little wonder that such persons feared abolitionists as med-
dlesome outsiders who undermined their local authority, as
faceless, power-hungry men who schemed from afar to intrude
into their personal affairs. Since the tactics of moral suasion
appealed directly to all persons — men, women, and children,
black as well as white — abolitionists paid no heed to local leadership and challenged traditional male prerogatives to speak
exclusively for their female and juvenile dependents. Boston's "aristocratic" champion of anti-abolitionism, the "blue-
blooded" Harrison Gray Otis, summarized all these resentments when warning of a "dangerous association" organized
"from afar . . . *a revolutionary society* — combined with auxilliary
societies in every state and community" that incited blacks to

violence, enticed women to "turn their sewing parties into abolition clubs," and seduced small children into defying their
parents with "gifts of sugar plums."
The social profile of the leading white immediatists substan-
tiated Otis's fears. While mobs were led by local "squires,"
most abolitionists came from less distinguished Protestant
stock. Indeed, some must have seemed to their opponents like
rootless outsiders, for recently emigrated Englishmen were often attracted to the movement. In religion, of course, the abolitionists' evangelicalism stood in sharp contrast to the
religious elitism of their upper-class foes. Many male abolitionists seemed to be far more versatile (if less wealthy) than the
"gentlemen of property and standing." They included a high
percentage of farmers, manufacturers, tradesmen, and artisans — men whose careers required skills consistent with the
emerging cosmopolitan economy but put little value on tradi-
tionally determined status. In practically every respect, white
abolitionist leadership embodied a cosmopolitanism that left
them unimpressed with their opponents' appeals to tradition
and local privilege.
As the "gentlemen of property and standing" united against
abolitionist threats, they quickly discovered how much they
had in common with the planters and lesser whites of the slave
states, and even with their working-class neighbors. For all
their obvious differences, members of these groups prized most
highly the male prerogative to rule over women, children, and
black people — groups in the North which abolitionists were
eager to reach. In the 1850s, during sporadic renewals of anti-
abolitionist violence, working-class Irish Catholic immigrants
demonstrated exactly these concerns. Though completely dis-
interested in the traditions of Yankee "aristocrats" or the
customs of the plantation, these newly arrived Irish men also
jealously guarded their authority over presumed inferiors.

By the mid-1830s, the enemies of abolition knew full well that the movement they so hated was becoming ever more formidable and far-flung. By the end of 1834, white men of great financial power and expertise like the Tappan brothers had taken control of the American Anti-Slavery Society in New York City. Lewis Tappan, Joshua Leavitt, and especially the Society's Corresponding Secretary, Elizur Wright, Jr., commanded bureaucratic skills exceptional in any era. They commissioned, paid, and equipped the many agents who successfully organized local societies throughout the North that served as efficient auxiliaries to the remote but seemingly all-powerful parent body in New York City.

Next, abolitionists implemented a series of impressive measures designed to reshape the nation's "climate of opinion." By 1834, *The Liberator*, under Garrison's sole control, had been joined by a battery of new publications that seemed to reach all corners of the North. Abolitionists now plunged wholeheartedly into mass communications, with highly venturesome women as well as men trafficking aggressively in "the marketplace of ideas." *The Emancipator*, published in New York and aiming at a national circulation, spoke officially for its sponsor, the American Anti-Slavery Society. By 1836 in Cincinnati, James G. Birney braved mob assaults as he struggled to get out copies of his weekly *Philanthropist*. The flow of illustrated periodicals bearing titles like *The Anti-Slavery Reporter, The Slave's Friend* (published by women for juvenile readers), and *Human Rights* suddenly seemed endless. Talented polemicists like William Jay, Elizur Wright, Jr., and Amos A. Phelps also availed themselves of the steam-driven press to publish powerful antislavery pamphlets. When Lydia Maria Child and Angelina Grimké contributed unqualified attacks on slavery and discrimination, critics cited this proof that "insolent" women were now daring in public to censure male behavior while pursuing the goal of "race amalgamation." White racism and male supremacy, both implicit in anti-abolitionist ideology, began openly to reinforce each other.

As a culmination of these endeavors, the American Anti-Slavery Society embarked on a new project in May 1835. Its aim, as Lewis Tappan put it, was "to sow the good seed of abolition thoroughly over the whole country," to flood every town and hamlet, North and South, with mailings of abolitionist literature. "The great postal campaign," as the abolitionists referred to it, set off a momentous reaction of mob activity in the North, repression in the South, and controversy in Congress. At the same time, this daring endeavor and the uproar it provoked began to persuade hitherto-uncommitted people to adopt an antislavery stance.

With an initial budget of thirty thousand dollars, the postal campaign turned out to be a pamphleteering effort of unprecedented proportions. Ministers, elected officials, and newspaper editors in every state, especially in the South, were placed on the mailing lists. Slaves and Southern free blacks, contrary to anti-abolitionist charges, were not. One by one, lifelong slaveholders would repent, the abolitionists expected, because they would realize that hostile world opinion was "a feeling against which they cannot stand." After freeing their slaves, these Southern manumissionists would then add their rebukes against those who continued to "ply the lash." Unrealistic as they were, these were the goals of the "great postal campaign." By the end of 1837, the American Anti-Slavery Society had posted over a million pieces of antislavery literature. In the interval, hysteria swept through the white South. Major Northern cities and small towns witnessed riotous mobs. Northern state legislatures and even Congress had begun debating measures to curtail antislavery agitation. The number of antislavery societies in the North had also mushroomed. A failure when judged by its own goals, the postal campaign nevertheless transformed abolitionism into a subject that no American could easily ignore. The Southern reaction, swift and severe, took the abolitionists aback. It also doomed their hopes of peacefully converting the slaveholder. Just after the mail from New York arrived, on July 29, 1835, angry South Carolinians broke into the Charleston post office and hauled away the satchels. The next evening, the mob reassembled and hung effigies of Garrison and Arthur Tappan. These were then consumed by a bonfire fueled by abolitionist newspapers. Leading planters organized vigilance societies to search the incoming mail and confiscate "incendiary literature." "The indications are that the South is unanimous in their resistance," John C. Calhoun announced, correctly. Clerics and congressmen throughout the slave states thundered against depraved Yankee conspirators. Everywhere in the South, free blacks, feared by whites as the chief targets of abolitionist plans for race war, faced ever more systematic repression, even reenslavement. President Andrew Jackson made known his approval of the white Southerners' behavior. In his 1836 Annual Message to Congress, Jackson decried the postal campaign and urged Congress to ban antislavery literature from the United States mails. Soon, several Southern state legislatures passed resolutions addressed to Northern state governments which called for laws to silence abolitionism. Connecticut responded with its famous 1836 "gag law" attempting to ban roving abolitionist speakers. No other Northern legislature complied, but their own denunciations of abolitionism encouraged the "gentlemen of property and standing" to take personal action. So, undoubtedly, did the success of Southern resistance and the uninhibited comments of the President of the United States.

Autumn 1835 saw anti-abolitionists all over the North creating violent uproar. Cadres of leading citizens began taking reprisals, usually directed at local gatherings of abolitionists and at the editors of antislavery newspapers. In a few instances, mob violence was spontaneous, but the far more typical anti-abolitionist riot was planned in advance and led by the local elites. In the Utica riot of October 1835, the pillars of the community took the lead against outside agitators as lawyers, politicians, merchants, and bankers, joined by a crowd of day laborers, broke up a state convention of abolitionists and roughed up several delegates. The Cincinnati mobs which repeatedly attacked James G. Birney's press were similar. In Philadelphia and Boston, where mobs attacked racially integrated gatherings of abolitionist women, the motives of the rioters in defending both male and white supremacy were particularly clear.

To abolitionists, and to many other worried citizens, violence seemed pervasive. Lydia Maria Child, like other abolitionists, imagined herself passing through scenes like those "of the French Revolution, when no man dared trust his neighbors." As the British abolitionist George Thompson and Garrison made their way from meeting to meeting, mobs greeted them at nearly every stop. In Boston in October 1835, a mob looking for "the English amalgamationist" Thompson stumbled instead upon Garrison and dragged him through the streets. Outside New England, abolitionist agents fared no better. Henry B. Stanton, operating in Ohio and Pennsylvania, estimated that he faced mobs on more than seventy occasions.

The most frightening scenes transpired in Alton, a small river town in extreme southern Illinois. In late 1837 the city's leaders finally lost all patience with Elijah P. Lovejoy, an "intruder" from Maine who edited *The Observer*, a newspaper equally uncompromising in its anti-Catholicism and antislavery. Prominent citizens made clear their unwillingness to protect Lovejoy from harm. He and his supporters refused to be cowed, even after mobs had twice thrown his press into the Mississippi River. On November 7, 1837, a mob again gathered, this time around the warehouse where Lovejoy and his adherents, armed, were guarding yet another press. They set the building afire. As Lovejoy rushed from the burning building, gun in hand, he was stopped by a bullet. Anti-abolitionist violence, which had until now focused on destroying property, had culminated in murder. Though deeply shaken, immediatists counted their first "martyr."

The wave of terrorism finally subsided in 1838; it had ironic but significant results. Every attempt to silence the abolitionists only drew attention to the movement, publicized its principles, and spread concern about civil liberties. From the first, the abolitionists exploited this fact, transforming mob action into a vehicle for moral suasion. "How the heathen rage!" wrote an exultant Samuel J. May to Garrison during the height of the violence. "Our opposers are doing everything to help us." Never before, he thought, had any subject been "ever so much talked about as slavery is everywhere." Abolitionists marked with satisfaction the ringing debates on slavery in newspapers and legislatures which accompanied the censorship proposals and the riot reports. "The cause is progressing," John Greenleaf Whittier decided. "I want no better evidence of it than the rabid violence of our enemies."

Even as abolitionists reassured one another about the benefits of repression, they also began to draw more sophisticated conclusions. The pervasiveness of anti-abolitionism cast grave doubts on their first perception of a nation ready to respond to "truth," and on their expectation that moral suasion would inaugurate a new era of national harmony and interracial brotherhood. In late 1837, Garrison expressed the frustration which had overtaken the movement. "When we first unfurled the banner of *The Liberator*," he wrote, "we did not anticipate that, in order to protect southern slavery, the free states would voluntarily trample under foot all order, law and government, or brand the advocates of universal liberty as incendiaries."

Judged by its initial aims, moral suasion had failed utterly; yet the opposition it had provoked was opening new possibilities, suggesting new tactics and new goals. Discouraging as it was, repression nonetheless did make some genuine converts. More important, it was helping to create a broad constituency of antislavery sympathizers who blamed violence-prone "southern influences" in the North for jeopardizing civil liberties. By the late 1830s, none could deny that, despite their failures, the abolitionists were beginning to make slavery an unavoidable issue in American political life.

4

PERFECTIONISM AND POLITICS

Albert Gallatin Riddle, a seasoned antislavery activist in northern Ohio, was always ready to share his observations on local matters. In 1842, he reported to Joshua Giddings, his congressional representative in Washington, that a "wide and deep feeling" of antagonism against the South "was silently stealing upon the hearts of our people." Mention "the question of Southern dictation," he declared, "and you see their eyes flash." This attitude, many abolitionists agreed, was the most heartening result of the violent 1830s. By the end of the decade, their programs of agitation and the repressive acts of their opponents had the combined effect of creating partially committed sympathizers like the ones Riddle described. These important constituencies, concentrated within clear geographic boundaries, became centers for abolitionism and breeding grounds for sectional impulses in American politics. By 1840, 2.5 million black Southerners seemed as far as ever from freedom. Yet abolitionists could measure definite though ambiguous "progress" in influential parts of the North.

The most easy-to-document gains were actual conversions to immediatism. Mob actions not only created sympathy for abolitionist victims but brought important new leaders into the

movement. Philanthropist Gerrit Smith, for example, had successfully resisted the combined moral suasion of Theodore D.
Weld, Lewis Tappan, and James G. Birney. But following the
Utica riot, which took place near his estate, Smith joined
the immediatists. Edmund Quincy dated his conversion to the
mobbing of Garrison. Yet it is clear that violent events provided only the occasion for these commitments, not the causes.
Most Americans who witnessed the mobs left without display-
ing the remotest interest in immediatism.

The individuals who "converted" in response to the mobs
had already demonstrated some reservations about slavery as
they struggled with deeper personal uncertainties. Wendell
Phillips, for example, was blessed with wealth, a keen mind,
rhetorical brilliance, striking good looks, and two degrees from
Harvard. Expected to join the Massachusetts Whig elite, he
displayed no enthusiasm for his glowing prospects as he hap-
hazardly practiced law during the mid-1830s. Witnessing the
1835 Garrison mob in Boston, Phillips felt disturbed, but was
"puzzled rather than astounded," and remained uncommitted.
By late 1837, however, he had defied his domineering mother
by impulsively marrying the brilliant but chronically infirm
Ann Terry Greene, an abolitionist, to whom he had proposed
on what all mistakenly had agreed was her deathbed. In the
midst of this emotional upheaval, Phillips heard the news of
the Alton riots and his indecision vanished: "The gun which
was aimed at the breast of Lovejoy . . . brought me to my
feet."

For the rest of his life, Phillips put his enormous talent for
public speaking and his considerable intellect behind immediatism, women's rights, and other radical causes. A remarkable
"aristocrat" who inspired reformers instead of mobbing them,
Phillips illustrates the danger of attempting to explain the abolitionists' motives by any single socioeconomic formula. The
same can be said of Garrison, whose impoverished origins

contrasted so markedly with Phillips's privileged upbringing. Important as they were, commitments like Smith's and Phillips's shrink in significance when compared with the widening spread of strong antislavery attitudes throughout whole regions of the North. Again, anti-abolitionist violence and Southern repression provided the catalyst. The disrupted meetings, the mail searches, the wrecked newspaper offices, and, above all, the murder of Lovejoy began to make many Northerners, abolitionists and non-abolitionists alike, wonder about the safety of America's civil liberties. Ordinary citizens who deplored the mobs began to suspect that slaveholders harbored contempt for the constitutionally guaranteed freedoms of all Americans to assemble peacefully and express their opinions.

Riot and repression also suggested that the planter class exercised a relentless dominance over political life in the North. "Gentlemen of property and standing" and "turbulent" workingmen seemed all too eager to do the bidding of slaveholding tyrants in crushing the freedoms of their abolitionist neighbors. As Birney once put it: "Whilst our aristocracy would preserve the domestic peace of the South, they seem totally to disregard the domestic peace of the North." This belief marked the origin of a compelling ideological formulation, the "slave-power conspiracy," to which Northerners subscribed in ever-increasing numbers as sectional conflicts multiplied and civil war drew closer.

Antislavery and pro-slavery feelings thus fed off one another. Supporters as well as opponents of abolition grew more numerous as each movement compounded fears of conspiracy on the part of its opponents, which then seemed confirmed by subsequent events. Many who were not abolitionists as well as all who were began to suspect that repression was transforming all of America's most precious freedoms into "hollow counterfeits." "FREE!" Theodore D. Weld exploded upon hearing of Lovejoy's death. "The word and the sounds are omnipresent masks and mockers. An impious lie unless they stand for free Lynch Law, and free murder; for they are free."

For ordinary Northerners who felt as Weld did, concern for civil rights rapidly merged with a general endorsement of some of the abolitionists' fundamental principles. To be sure, immediatists were careful to distinguish themselves, the "true" abolitionists, from whites who worried about their own liberty, but not necessarily about the freedom of the slave. Some historians have also insisted on a sharp distinction between anti-Southern feelings which tolerated slavery and racism and the radical doctrines of immediate abolitionism.

While instructive, the distinction can also be misleading, especially in assessing abolitionism's political impact. For one thing, slaveholders never bothered with such fine points. Many immediate abolitionists showed no less concern than did other white Northerners about the fate of the nation's "precious legacies of freedom." The idea that emancipation would salvage the hard-won rights of all Americans inspired a rich theme of republican ideology that had always suffused immediatist thought. As Birney once put it: "The liberties of those yet free are in imminent peril . . . It is not only for the emancipation of the enslaved that we contend."

Immediatism became most difficult to distinguish from broader anti-Southern opinions once ordinary citizens began articulating these intertwining beliefs. Occupationally versatile, evangelically inspired men had shown an inclination to embrace immediatism, and some of the same social traits seem to apply in regions where anti-Southern political feelings suddenly appeared. As repression continued and political controversy grew, northern Ohio's Western Reserve, Indiana's northernmost counties, parts of eastern Michigan, upstate New York, portions of western Vermont, and western Massachusetts became rural hotbeds of anti-Southern politics and centers of abolitionist recruitment.

Although settled at widely separate times, each of these regions had been founded by Puritan New Englanders. Usually of ordinary backgrounds, these transplanted Yankees had carried with them pronounced preferences for family farming, evangelical religion, and New England institutions, just as did many immediatists. From the early 1830s to the early 1840s, homogeneous Protestant populations still dominated, but momentous economic developments were overtaking these areas. Each was being transformed from a cluster of backcountry hamlets and isolated homesteads into centers of cash-crop agriculture and commercial enterprise. In the territory which ultimately extended from eastern Michigan and northern Ohio through upstate New York, recently opened canals and a burgeoning lake-shipping trade stimulated regional interdependence. New urban markets were created which ran from Detroit and Cleveland through Erie, Rochester, and Syracuse to Utica and Albany. By the mid-1830s, vastly improved water and land routes had also linked what were to become the antislavery regions of rural Vermont, New Hampshire, and Massachusetts to urban centers.

Washtenaw, Michigan; Oswego, New York; Ashtabula, Ohio; Pittsfield, Massachusetts; and Dover, New Hampshire are representative of the many crossroad villages in the North which had transformed themselves into important commercial centers and into beehives of abolitionism. Serving the cash-crop farmers in the hinterland, newspapers proliferated in these smaller towns, creating sophisticated networks of communication. These, in turn, ensured citizens' heightened involvement in national issues, such as the mobbing of abolitionists and the ransacking of mailbags. Unusually large concentrations of public schools and private academies encouraged children to confront moral controversy while providing skills essential to economic success in this dynamic region.

The parents of such children held fast to the importance of

individual enterprise and the promise of social mobility. Material and moral progress, they firmly believed, depended on the efforts of "free laborers"—self-employed farmers, artisans, and workers. So did the other hallmarks of a "civilized" society—evangelical piety, family stability, republican governance, and the diffusion of secular knowledge. All were indistinguishable parts of God's benevolent plans. Judged against these values, the ethos of the plantation and the repression of the abolitionists seemed disturbingly related expressions of unchecked slaveholding power. For what did the planter class seem to embody, after all, but the most fundamental denial of their "free labor" ideals? Searching for the cause of the melees which had erupted in and around their orderly communities, many Northerners, artisans, commercial farmers, and entrepreneurs foremost among them, fixed upon the slaveholders.

Perceived by suspicious Northerners as parasitic exploiters of at least two million slaves, the planter class stood condemned as the corrupted custodians of their own perverted interests. All other Southern whites—impoverished, ignorant victims of this retrograde aristocracy—were seen as being rendered listless, mute, and helpless. Instead of building stable families and enforcing strict morality, the planters, debauched by idleness, were believed to vent their unbridled lusts in the gaming rooms, at the race tracks, in the taverns, and especially late at night among defenseless women in the slave quarters. The excess of this polluted South, it seemed to hostile Northerners, now threatened the very fabric of their own society. Gerrit Smith, from the heart of upstate New York's "Burnt-Over District," articulated his neighbors' misgivings when he announced in 1836 that Northerners must now oppose slavery "in self defense." He warned that the planter class, "if it not be overthrown," would continue in its "aggression . . . and effectually prepare the way for reducing northern laborers into a herd of slaves."

Abolitionists understood the general characteristics of this emerging antislavery constituency and quickly took steps to encourage its progress. Increasingly sensitive to the opinions of independent farmers and entrepreneurs, what Elizur Wright, Jr., described as the "small men" of the towns and countryside, besieged abolitionists like James G. Birney advised a hostile critic in late 1835 that the mobs would fail to silence the abolitionists. "We have only to fly to the country," Birney asserted, "to be welcomed by the warm and honest hearts of our yeomanry, and by the artisans and inhabitants of the smaller villages." Accordingly, abolitionists also began to concentrate their campaigns in these centers of rural capitalism. For example, the seventy agents dispatched under Theodore D. Weld's direction by the American Anti-Slavery Society focused their efforts between 1835 and 1837 in northern Ohio and upstate New York. The Massachusetts Anti-Slavery Society likewise concentrated on that state's western regions.

As these new constituencies voiced their concerns, abolitionists moved to translate them into direct expressions of antislavery through an aggressive petition campaign. Legislative petitions had constituted a vital part of the Northern emancipation movement in the eighteenth century, and antislavery requests to governmental bodies from both African Americans and whites had continued into the 1820s. Sensitive to these precedents, the Declaration of Sentiments of the American Anti-Slavery Society had pledged abolitionists to instruct legislatures by affixing their names to petitions. Even before the start of their national petition campaign, immediatists had forwarded to Congress requests for the abolition of slavery in the District of Columbia and the interstate slave trade as well as protests against the admission of new slave states.

By late 1835, the volume of antislavery petitions had provoked controversy on the floor of Congress. The next year the number of petition signatures rose to over thirty thousand;

sectional debates in the House of Representatives grew increasingly intemperate. Then, in May of 1837, the American Anti-Slavery Society announced plans for a still more concentrated national effort which relied on volunteers all over the North to circulate petitions among their friends and neighbors.

The importance of local initiative, community involvement, and the individual act of affixing one's signature to an anti-slavery protest is impossible to overstress. By making this gesture, unprecedented numbers of people found a safe yet politically effective way to express their sympathy for abolitionism and their hostility toward the South. Most petitions were taken from door to door by local volunteers who turned agitation into an expression of neighborly interest. The petitions themselves, especially those regarding the ending of slavery in the District of Columbia and the ban on admitting new slave states, were drawn up so that all people suspicious of Southern institutions, not just committed immediatists, could sign them. In sectionally conscious neighborhoods, these were subjects upon which, as Elizur Wright, Jr., put it, "all classes, Abolitionists, Colonizationists, Mongrels, and Nothingarians can agree." In addition, petitions were often phrased in supplicating biblical terms, deferential tones that assured hesitant women signatories that they remained in their traditional gender "sphere" even as they "intruded" into the political process.

Attracted by the campaign's neighborly approach and benign political style, women took the lead in circulating petitions, signing them, and sending out the forms. In the process they began developing self-confidence, political consciousness, and administrative skill that could inspire more extensive activism. Male abolitionists, unaware of the deeper significance of such activities, warmly encouraged them. "If the ladies . . . really take the business in hand, it will go," Garrison exclaimed. Lydia Maria Child, Elizabeth Cady (soon to marry Henry B. Stanton), Lucretia Mott, and a very young Susan B.

Anthony took the challenge to heart and successfully tested their leadership and managerial expertise. In smaller towns and farmsteads, thousands of less than famous women did likewise, overseen by the many female antislavery societies created since the early 1830s. Over half the petitions bore women's signatures, a fact which indicates the strong connection between the petition campaign and the soon-to-emerge debate within abolitionism over women's rights. "It is meet that the maids and matrons . . . should take the lead in this matter," Garrison gibed in 1836, "but what are the men doing?"

By May 1838, after one year of intensive effort, the American Anti-Slavery Society reported, an astonishing 415,000 petitions had been forwarded to Washington. Almost two years earlier, well before it found itself deluged by this tide of remonstrance, the House of Representatives had voted that antislavery petitions could not be the subject of parliamentary debate. When received, they were automatically tabled. Passed during the height of anti-abolitionist violence and in force until late 1844, this was the famous gag rule which was to play such an influential role in sectionalizing American politics and in politicizing abolitionism.

Complex motives and political dealings lay behind the enactment of the gag rule. Some militant slaveholders agitated for an even stronger measure, hoping that the abolitionists' outrage at such a bill would further harden the position of the white South. Understandably, slaveowning representatives deeply resented petitions which called their way of life an abomination and which proposed measures detrimental to their interests. Southern politicians had long before concluded that all discussion of slavery, whether in mailed pamphlets or on the floor of Congress, posed a grievous threat to the institution. And all politicians, Whig and Democrat alike, knew that arguments over slavery generated sectional hostility, weakened party structures, and threatened the Union.

Given this diverse array of interests and convictions, Congress still managed to pass a gag rule that satisfied all slaveholders, nearly all Northern Democrats, and most Northern Whigs. In response, abolitionists redoubled their petitioning, inaugurating an impressive national campaign in 1837. The number of signers jumped dramatically, for the gag rule only added force to abolitionists' warnings that plantation despots connived with "Northern men with Southern principles" to strengthen slavery at the expense of all constitutionally guaranteed liberties. The right of petition, along with the rights of free speech, free assembly, and the free press, was collapsing under the blows of "slave power."

The repercussions of the gag rule were quickly apparent. In the House of Representatives, former President John Quincy Adams, now a Whig congressman from Massachusetts, rose in 1837 to defend the right of petition and freedom of debate. Aged, acerbic, and embittered by his conviction that slaveholders had prevented his reelection to the Presidency, "Old Man Eloquent" constantly offered petitions in defiance of the gag rule and thrust the subject of slavery into debate whenever possible. Since Adams enjoyed continuous support from his constituents, he became the recipient of antislavery petitions from all over the North; nearly every other congressman refused to present even those from their own districts. In the late 1830s, however, several new Whig congressmen joined Adams, notably Joshua R. Giddings from Ohio's Western Reserve, Seth Gates from New York's "Burnt-Over District," and William Slade from a heavily "abolitionized" district in Vermont.

The arrival of these men in Washington marked a fateful turning point in American politics, fraught with implications for abolitionists, for slaveholders and slaves, for politicians of all varieties, indeed for the entire generation that witnessed the coming of the Civil War. The self-propelling cycle of agitation and repression had created important pockets of Northern voters who insisted that their elected representatives articulate their stern opposition to slaveholding, to violations of civil rights, and to the behavior and values of the planter class. In utter opposition to the prevailing intersectional consensus, these politicians had a mandate to debate the morality of slavery, openly and often, regardless of party discipline. Giddings, for example, ran for his first term in Congress on a platform which decried the institution of slavery in general, and in particular the gag rule, the slave trade between the states, and slaveholding in the District of Columbia. The Ashtabula County Anti-Slavery Society (organized with the aid of Theodore D. Weld) expressed pleasure at Giddings's "manly and independent stand," and he handily won the first of nine consecutive terms to Congress. Self-educated, politically ambitious, and from a poverty-stricken Calvinist family with Connecticut roots, Giddings, in succeeding as an attorney and land speculator, exemplified the rising social status so commonly found in the broad antislavery movement. As if to emphasize his social position, Giddings chose as his law partner Benjamin Franklin Wade, another poor Connecticut farm boy who had arrived in the Western Reserve as a member of a canal-digging crew. By 1851, Wade had taken his seat in the United States Senate, as blunt-spoken a foe of the planter class as Giddings.

As the sectional crisis deepened during the 1840s and 1850s, many other politicians with similar backgrounds came to power, relying on the issue of slavery to make their mark in politics. Renegade Democrats like John P. Hale of New Hampshire, Salmon P. Chase of Ohio, Preston King of New York, and David Wilmot of Pennsylvania, as well as dissident Whigs such as Henry Wilson of Massachusetts, George W. Julian of Indiana (later Giddings's son-in-law), Thaddeus Stevens of Pennsylvania, and, certainly, Abraham Lincoln, could justly claim to be self-made men. Belief in the nobility of free labor, self-education, and economic independence was central to the careers of each of these men as they battled "slave power" over the next two decades. The more the voters supported such politicians, the more difficult it became for traditional parties to contain sectional disruption. Giddings demonstrated this in 1842 by resigning after being censured congressionally for his antislavery activities. Rushing home to the Western Reserve, he stood for reelection and was sent back to Washington by a huge majority.

Sectional debates in politics and the abolitionists' petition campaigns both received enormous stimulus in 1835 when Congress found itself debating the most volatile sectional issue of all — the question of slavery's westward expansion. Independent Texas, with a slaveholding constitution, had broken away from Mexico several years earlier. As the political leaders of this enormous slaveholding area now petitioned for its annexation by the United States, antislavery-minded citizens everywhere protested. Congressmen like Adams and Giddings vowed to resist any territorial expansion that would strengthen the plantation economy and augment the slaveholders' political power.

The same tensions which had accompanied the admission of Missouri some fifteen years earlier were reemerging, this time in far more volatile form. The new two-party system depended entirely on broad voter participation and mass political awareness. By the 1830s, the telegraph, the steam press, and the mass-produced newspaper, not to mention universal male suffrage, knit relationships between governors and the governed more closely than ever before. Though the two-party system depended heavily on sectional compromise, these instruments of mass politics also guaranteed that frictions between North and South generated by politicians in Washington would rapidly be communicated to the public-at-large. By a reverse application of the same process, the agitation of abolitionists on the local level of politics registered quickly and strongly in the deliberations of Congress and the actions of party leaders.

Here was an environment in which sectional ideologues like John C. Calhoun and John Quincy Adams could exercise a highly disproportionate influence. Adams, Giddings, and other Whigs repeatedly warned in widely reprinted speeches that annexation meant more Southern congressmen to vote for the gag rule, as well as a new market for slave-dealers in the upper South that would fortify the plantation economy against the inroads of free labor. In sum, they argued, the annexation of Texas cushioned the Southern economy's deepest internal weaknesses, creating an even greater, more aggressive "slave power." Southern politicians responded that the Constitution guaranteed slaveholders a full share in westward expansion, as demonstrated when Tennessee, Kentucky, Louisiana, and Missouri had joined the Union.

Sectionalizing trends that mirrored the direction of politics also influenced the abolitionists, as indicated in the goals of their petition campaign. Abolitionists had envisioned their petitions as a means of changing national attitudes about slavery. But their efforts now focused exclusively northward. While most reformers still desired that "the pure and peaceable" principles of abolition would yet "overspread the South," it was clear by 1837 that immediatism only intensified racial and sectional discord; it was hardly the soothing balm first imagined. If anything, the white South was more united and the institution of slavery better guarded than ever before. Garrison's prophecy that moral suasion would soon make black skin "popular" had proven a sad mockery.

Yet the petition campaign was proving successful in ways that abolitionists had not foreseen. Increasing numbers of ordinary Northerners began registering their deep conviction that slaveowning jeopardized their civil rights, disturbed their domestic tranquillity, and insulted their codes of morality. This development was ripe with antislavery potential. Yet these attitudes also contained ambiguities which all reformers were obliged to ponder. For one thing, antislavery feelings such as these were easy to harmonize with race prejudice. People who adopted such views, moreover, though sometimes sympathetic to ending slavery, usually remained suspicious of Garrison, Tappan, Weld, and their colleagues.

As abolitionists pondered these confusing trends and reflected on the failures of moral suasion, they found themselves forced to consider new tactics and formulate new goals. What did the repression signify? How as Christians should they respond to it and to other forms of coercion? In light of their recent experiences, what should their posture be toward the unremitting hostility of religious denominations and political parties? How should they respond to antislavery feelings among Northerners who nonetheless rejected immediatism? These critical problems generated deep ideological conflict, and by mid-1837 deep factional discord had begun to disrupt the American Anti-Slavery Society. By 1840, abolitionist unity had vanished forever.

More than anyone else, William Lloyd Garrison and Angelina Grimké provoked the initial conflicts that finally shattered the movement. As early as 1835, Arthur Tappan had reacted sharply to Garrison's harsh anticlerical attacks on orthodox New England Calvinists. But by late 1837 it seemed to many beside Tappan that the Boston editor had given himself over completely to doctrinal extremism. Now he counted among his closest confidants Angelina Grimké and her sister Sarah, restless women from South Carolina who had fled their slaveholding family to defy their "appointed female sphere" and to oppose slavery by speaking as immediatists before male audiences. In widely circulated writings, they also dared to reject the authority of ministers, question the literal truth of Scripture, criticize the coercive power of the state, and demand equality for women. Garrison not only endorsed these novel ideas but eagerly expanded them to encompass a sweeping denial of all governmental authority and a religious belief in human perfectibility.

There were many reasons for this explosion of radicalism within the movement. The anti-authoritarian tenor of abolitionism certainly pushed some abolitionists ever further along paths of personal discovery and spiritual self-transformation. The immorality of slaveholding could suggest troubling analogies with one's most personal relationships and loyalties. Submission to the worldly discipline of governments, political parties, ministers, patriarchical husbands, or even to one's own private passions seemed to some abolitionists disturbingly linked to the exploitation of black human beings.

Garrison, for example, found confirmation for his developing non-resistance theories in 1837 after conversations with John Humphrey Noyes, a utopian socialist who had condemned civil government and marriage contracts as the equivalent of holding slaves or butchering American Indians. Angelina Grimké followed a similar logic and consulted with Garrison when conflating male dominance and racial slavery as related forms of sexual and spiritual exploitation. As abolitionists molded their deepest personal misgivings into frightening images of slaveholding, their goals of self-sanctification, slave emancipation, and social revolution could become wholly intertwined.

Yet the emergence of religious iconoclasm and women's rights must also be explained in the context of white abolitionists' recent experiences as reformers. For the spiritually questing Angelina Grimké (detractors dubbed her "Devilina"), abolitionist feminism derived as much from her memories of living amid slavery, the abuse she and others encountered as immediatists, and the blossoming of her oratorical powers, as it did from her growing spirituality. The petition campaign's widespread mobilization of abolitionist women also explains why the Grimkés felt moved to espouse women's rights when they did. In much the same fashion, Garrison and his supporters embraced Christian non-resistance, gender equality, and anti-governmentalism only after reflecting on the meaning of anti-abolitionist repression and reaching deeply negative conclusions about prevailing American values. To these incipient radicals, violence, gag rules, mail looting, and denunciations from every religious denomination revealed an infamy which had overtaken North and South alike, which could be overcome only by transforming every white American's institutional loyalties and system of beliefs. "Moral suasion," they now insisted, meant "moral revolution."

Unlike many of the immediatists who were soon to oppose them, Garrison and his supporters put little emphasis on the value of repression in gaining sympathy for the cause. They concluded that the country deserved, as Garrison wrote, "an avalanche of wrath, hurled from the Throne of God, to crush us into annihilation." American Christianity, "mean, dwarfed and corrupt," relied on "armed hosts" and engaged in "bloody strife to avenge the slightest threat offered to its dignity" by the abolitionists. In Garrison's opinion, Northern Whigs and Democrats, clear barometers of majority opinion, had reacted much as the mobs and the churches had, "striving to see who will show the most hatred toward us . . . in order to win southern votes." He now believed that mass opinion, directing the power of church and state, was fostering huge perversions of God's will. Illustrating the same process, a despairing Angelina Grimké recoiled at the news of Lovejoy's murder and declared herself a non-resistant. To her, as well as to Garrison, it seemed obvious that appeals to conscience had to be expanded to induce a total reshaping of the nation's ethical values and institutional practices and a peaceful revolution to transform every facet of American life. By 1838, Garrison, the Grimkés, and many other influential immediatists were embracing such "fanatical" principles. With these heretical ideas came unconventional people who could easily be taken for fanatics. To be sure, several of Garrison's closest associates — Edmund Quincy, Wendell Phillips, and Maria Weston Chapman — exuded aristocratic refinement. But there was also Charles Calistius Burleigh, a close associate of Garrison's, who sported cascading golden curls, a flowing beard, and robes like an Old Testament prophet's. Others of Garrison's circle like Parker Pillsbury, Nathaniel P. Rogers, and Stephen S. Foster were highly disruptive practitioners of moral suasion. In addition to the Grimkés, critics also pointed to Lucretia Mott, Abby Kelley (who would marry Stephen S. Foster in 1845), Maria Weston Chapman, and Elizabeth Cady Stanton, who scorned women's "appointed spheres" and demanded equality within the antislavery societies. By 1838, it appeared to many in the movement and outside it that abolitionism was being overrun by dreamers and cranks.

The leaders who most bridled at "Garrisonism" were the administratively talented white men who had taken national responsibility for the postal and petition campaigns. Lewis Tappan, Joshua Leavitt, James G. Birney, Elizur Wright, Jr., John Greenleaf Whittier, and Henry B. Stanton were the most prominent. Garrison and most of his supporters had not been as deeply involved; they had participated but on lower levels.

Perhaps for this reason, Tappan, Birney, and other leading opponents of Garrison felt strongly that the battle for abolition was being waged within a healthy but seriously flawed society. They pointed to the thousands of conventional Northerners, suddenly sensitive to the evils of "slave power," who were signing petitions, resisting the annexation of Texas, and supporting the fight against the gag rule. It would be a tactical disaster, they thought, to confuse abolitionism with "extraneous" causes like women's rights and non-resistance. The new antislavery constituency just taking form would certainly recoil at such heresies. Moral suasion was coming to mean arousing a mass of reachable Northern men, religious or not. Meantime, Garrison and his colleagues had begun to espouse moral revolution on the totally opposite premise that the people's majoritarian values were actually the sources of chronic national disease. By 1838, disagreements about strategy and tactics, far too fundamental for compromise, had surfaced in the American Anti-Slavery Society.

Beyond these important struggles over strategies and personalities, the plain fact was that Garrison's beliefs repelled his opponents and threatened them personally. On the question of women's rights, for example, Lewis Tappan and James G. Birney stood fast for masculine dominance and agreed with Elizur Wright, Jr., when he remarked that the "tom turkies," not the hens, "ought to do the gobbling." Numerous abolitionist women agreed, upheld the "woman's sphere," and joined their evangelical husbands in condemning Garrison's anticlericalism as, in the words of Elizur Wright, Jr., "rankest infidelity . . . undermining the whole fabric of social relations." Garrison, for his part, criticized such opinions as evidence of moral atrophy. Inevitably, tensions between committed reformers and confirmed visionaries grew ever more pronounced.

From early 1838 until the breakup of the American Anti-Slavery Society in May 1840, conspiratorial designs and ideological conflict overshadowed all else in abolitionism. Garrison insisted that abolitionism retain a "broad platform," as he called it. All who pronounced slavery a sin and were dedicated to black equality should be welcomed into the American Anti-Slavery Society, regardless of their opinions on the Sabbath, women's rights, the validity of government, or any other subject. Intent on purging the anti-government, feminist radicals, leaders such as Henry B. Stanton and Elizur Wright, Jr., insisted, to the contrary, on a new, restrictive criterion. All true abolitionists had a moral duty to vote for Whig or Democratic Party candidates sympathetic to the cause. Direct political action should be the focus of abolitionist effort.

By attempting to transform the American Anti-Slavery Society into a political pressure group that required its members to vote, anti-Garrisonians clearly aimed to purge abolitionists who opposed involvement with government on religious grounds as well as those who insisted on women's right to the franchise. (Women were barred by law from the ballot box in every state.) Yet both the call to political action and Garrison's contrary espousals of Christian anarchism and women's rights were more than weapons in factional infighting. By the late 1830s, abolitionism clearly needed a fresh approach. With moral suasion in shambles, the continuous rounds of meetings, resolutions, and remonstrances now seemed soul-deadening and ineffectual. Garrison's zestful call for a revolutionary re-examination of human relationships and national values promised an imaginative new direction. So did the prospect of political activism.

If the indirect pressure of the petition campaign had stimulated so much new antislavery feeling in Congress, some anti-Garrisonians wondered, how much more might be gained by a forthright political movement? By 1838, some individuals had begun to talk about a third party based exclusively on abolitionist principles. But, whatever its form, any political effort meant attracting antislavery supporters who hardly considered themselves activists. Any association of an abolitionist political party with Garrisonism would obviously alienate potential voters.

In July 1840, warring factions of pro- and anti-Garrisonian delegates convened in New York City, intent on seizing or breaking up the American Anti-Slavery Society. Both sides packed the meeting, but antipolitical Garrisonians proved the superior political infighters. Abby Kelley, an unapologetic feminist, was elected to the executive committee, 557 to 451, and the defeated faction left the society forever. Garrison, not purged but triumphant, now presided over a truncated but far more radical body in which women and men had equal rights. Most on the losing side affiliated with Lewis Tappan's newly formed American and Foreign Anti-Slavery Society, although some like Theodore D. Weld rejected both factions as self-serving and morally bankrupt.

On state and local levels, the impact of the "great schism" varied, especially among women's groups. The Boston Female Anti-Slavery Society collapsed as a result of factional struggles nearly identical to those just described. In Philadelphia, female abolitionists avoided such divisions and maintained their society for another two decades. In smaller towns throughout New England and the Midwest, women's auxiliaries persisted among evangelicals, as did their petition campaigns, usually addressed to state and local issues of race reform. Neither needing nor wanting membership in separate societies, feminist abolitionists continued their activism in affiliates of the American Anti-Slavery Society, holding office and serving as lecturers and recruitment agents. As the controversy over women's rights spilled over into the 1840s, abolitionists of both genders could be found in every organization.

To African American activists, the fracturing of the American Anti-Slavery Society actually meant less than might first be supposed. Most prominent leaders initially felt reluctant to involve themselves, hoping instead, as one of them put it, that the whites would "bury the hatchet and do nothing to reflect [badly] on our holy cause in this our beloved though slave-ridden country." Some blacks did wonder how Garrison's call for voluntary self-disenfranchisement could assist African Americans in their quest for voting rights. Others questioned the pertinence to slave emancipation of religious perfectionism or equality for women. But when the moment arrived to declare allegiances, most blacks initially sided with Garrison, whom they respected highly.

The impact of the schism was also lessened because, as it took place, a new generation of African American activists was beginning to develop. The opening of the 1840s witnessed the passing of patriarchs like James Forten, Paul Cuffee, Richard Allen, and others whose leadership dated from the Revolution. Replacing them were young men like Forten's son-in-law, Robert Purvis, who had benefited greatly from an abolitionist education that had schooled him in immediatist doctrine and the ways of white reformers, and had given him the skills required for professional success. Soon to join him were Oberlin-educated people such as John Mercer Langston, and graduates of the extraordinary Oneida Institute, which over the next decade produced a galaxy of leaders. Fully integrated, supported by Tappan money, and with the irrepressible white evangelical Beriah Green as its superintendent, the Institute graduated, among others, Alexander Crummell, Jermain Loguen, and Henry Highland Garnett. These men, and prominent fugitives like Frederick Douglass who were to join them, would have far greater influence over black abolitionism than would ongoing arguments between the white reformers.

In national politics, meanwhile, where white men defined the issues, Northern concern over the expansion of the menacing "slave power" continued to deepen and spread. The sectional debates in Washington made it clear to all immediatists that politics and antislavery were rapidly merging. The antislavery constituency was now registering its feelings in Congress and at the ballot box, and would continue to do so on its own or in conjunction with the abolitionists. With some reluctance, some anti-Garrisonians began to plan the creation of a formal political organization, the Liberty Party, to offer authentic abolitionist alternatives in the election of 1840.

Garrisonians, in turn, admonished their apostate colleagues

that slavery and racism could never be overcome at the ballot box without a previous revolution in the moral values of the voters. Antislavery politicians, they warned, would inevitably compromise; winning elections would take precedence over freeing slaves. If, by chance, emancipation was enacted through a political process dominated by the unregenerate, race prejudice would certainly persist, turning black freedom into a cruel hoax. As it worked out, sectional conflicts in politics did intensify during the 1840s. Liberty Party leaders soon found themselves facing the task of converting antislavery politics into abolitionist politics. The extent of their success or failure measured the accuracy of Garrison's gloomy estimate of politicians as agents of emancipation.

5

THE POLITICS OF FREEDOM

August 1840 saw the Liberty Party campaigning hard for its emancipationist candidates. That same month, 130 black activists convened in Albany, New York, to launch a political crusade of their own. Vowing to "shake off the putrid garments of degradation," they announced the start of a "giant effort" to assert their political equality. In New York State, only the small number of African Americans who satisfied stringent property and residency requirements were permitted to vote. But these activists were demanding that the franchise be extended to include all black men living within the state. During the 1840s, abolitionists of both races plunged into politics on national and state levels, hoping to forward the cause of racial justice. All these crusaders were soon to discover just how intractable the political system could be.

Though politically inexperienced, the leaders of the Liberty Party were right to emphasize the novelty of their enterprise. Never before had a party had for its platform the imperative of abolishing slavery. Never had officeseekers so completely fused moral absolutes with vote-getting. Indeed, one can argue that the Liberty Party's was actually an "antipolitical" quest for reform no less religiously inspired than attempts to eliminate slavery and racism with sermons and tracts. Antebellum politics sought common ideological denominators, satisfying to broad and contradictory constituencies. By contrast, James G. Birney, Gerrit Smith, Joshua Leavitt, Henry B. Stanton, and others urged the citizenry to abandon the tainted Whigs and Democrats and "vote as you pray and pray as you vote."

For Liberty men, the Presidential election of 1840 did resemble a religious crusade by the sanctified against the depraved. The Democrats had renominated that notorious "tool of the slave power," Martin Van Buren, while the Whigs settled on William Henry Harrison, repugnant for Indian killing as well as for slaveholding. Liberty men harbored no expectations of victory for their "truly Christian candidate," James G. Birney. Rather, they hoped to attract enough supporters to achieve a balance of power between the two major parties as they enlightened the voters by condemning the sin of slavery.

The Liberty Party's creeds are significant because nearly all antislavery politicians eventually upheld them, though in much-moderated form. While endorsing the principle of immediatism, the party nevertheless denied that the federal government had the authority to abolish slavery in the states where it existed. Congress, however, could end slavery and the slave trade in the District of Columbia, terminate the interstate and coastwise slave trade, and bar the admission of new slave states to the Union. This states'-rights view, repugnant to all Southerners, was nevertheless the least extreme abolitionist theory. A smaller number of political abolitionists maintained that the congressional power of abolition extended into the slave states proper. By contrast, Garrisonian disunionists, who agreed completely with the slaveholders that the Constitution fully protected slavery, refused to vote and called for a dissolution of the Union. These theories, all marred by legal inconsistencies, reflected again the differences between Liberty men, who equated abolitionism with political purification, and Garrisonians, who glimpsed spiritual revolution.

For Liberty men, the problem of stimulating repentance quickly became complicated by the obvious fact that most antislavery voters preferred their accustomed parties. From the voters' point of view, the third party simply did not address economic issues of great concern to them, particularly those of tariffs, banking policy, internal improvements, and the sale of western lands. The presence in the Whig Party of men such as John Quincy Adams, Joshua Giddings, and Seth M. Gates indicated that strong opposition to slavery was quite compatible with membership in a national party that addressed all these other questions. Here was an appeal which the Liberty Party could never hope to equal as long as its platform spoke exclusively to the issue of slavery.

Despite these disadvantages, third-party organizers expected to have greatest success in regions where anti-Southern feelings already ran deep. In these districts the Liberty men began to offer complete slates of candidates, establish newspapers, and attack local Whigs and Democrats. Occasionally, as in the Massachusetts elections in the early 1840s, the third party was able to attract enough votes to hold a balance of power. Some Whig and Democratic politicians, then, began to make antislavery statements, hoping to lessen the Liberty Party's impact on their constituents. By forcing the major parties to adopt more emphatic antislavery positions, Liberty leaders were able to exert an influence above their meager numbers.

Perhaps no politician more aptly illustrated this dynamic than did Joshua R. Giddings. From 1840 to 1848, Giddings's Western Reserve congressional district had the largest concentration of Liberty Party voters in Ohio; his district also consistently delivered the heaviest Whig majorities of any in the state. Yet, early in the 1840s, Liberty men busied themselves in Giddings's stronghold, founding an ably edited newspaper and capturing the support of well-seasoned local politicians. On the state level, Giddings also began to encounter opposition from Gamaliel Bailey, a talented editor whose Cincinnati *Philanthropist* reflected Liberty Party opinion all over the Northwest. From New York City, meanwhile, came the pungent anti-Giddings sentiments of Joshua Leavitt, now editor of *The Emancipator* and a zealous third-party leader.

From these sources arose the charge that Giddings's Whig allegiance actually made him a sinful accessory to slavery, not the "friend of freedom" that he claimed to be. Third-party spokesmen cited Giddings's electioneering on behalf of the slaveowning William Henry Harrison, his votes for slaveholders as Speakers of the House of Representatives, and his refusal on constitutional grounds to support repeal of the 1793 Fugitive Slave Law. Voters in Ohio's sixteenth district were actually supporting slavery by casting their ballots for Giddings, Liberty Party spokesmen warned.

To counter these allegations, Giddings offered an increasingly sharp sectional argument, insisting that his antislavery principles justified his Whig loyalty. As early as 1840, editorials appeared over his signature which depicted Whig candidate Harrison as favorable to antislavery measures, such as ending the gag rule and abolishing slavery in the District of Columbia. Democrats like Van Buren were, on the other hand, completely subservient to the South, Giddings maintained, and only the Whig Party could act effectively against slavery. Liberty men hindered progress, he argued, for every vote cast for Birney aided the slavery-ridden Democrats by cutting into the Whig electorate.

As anti-Southern feeling mounted during the slavery-extension debates of the 1840s, Northern Whigs and Democrats increasingly made similar assertions. In the process, sectional neutrals and Southern politicians became aware of a terrible fact — the third party's antislavery challenge could not be met without allowing explosive sectional ideologies to circulate within the Northern branches of their parties. Giddings, Adams, William Slade, and the rest only intensified the process: in comparison to Liberty Party antagonists, they were perceived as moderates by voters. Their attitudes toward slavery, certainly radical by all standards of national politics, appeared restrained when compared with Liberty Party extremism. Duly elected agitators thus enjoyed the luxury of speaking as emphatically as they cared to. Suppose he should join the third party, Giddings once challenged a Liberty man, "what advantage could be gained? . . . Could I speak and act more freely, could I be more independent in the declaration of the principles of human rights?" The answer was, plainly, negative. While Liberty Party organizers never enjoyed victory at the ballot box, their local efforts gave enormous stimulus to antislavery feeling within the major parties.

In the early 1840s, however, Leavitt, Stanton, and other political abolitionists began to yearn for more satisfying polling results than the 7,056 votes the Liberty Party had attracted in the 1840 Presidential election. In that campaign, the Liberty Party's platform dealt only with the issue of slavery. After a serious depression befell the nation's economy in 1837, antislavery voters like other voters became increasingly anxious to know how candidates stood on banking, tariffs, and public-land policy. A party which was mute on these questions was fated to be ignored.

The Whigs encouraged voters to fix the blame for the economy on the Democrats, the party in power when depression took hold; antislavery Whigs also found a sectional variation of this tactic extremely useful in their struggle against the Liberty Party. The ruinous economic policies of the Democrats, they maintained, were the result of an exclusive dedication to forwarding the perverse interests of "slave labor." Protective tariffs, national banks, federally sponsored internal improvements, and equitable homestead laws, on the other hand, reflected the Whig commitment to the interests of "free labor" and "Northern rights." Their party's economic programs, such Whigs asserted, were as much antislavery measures as would be abolishing slavery in the District of Columbia or repealing the gag rule. Alongside such a versatile antislavery statement, the Liberty Party's one issue of abolition certainly appeared unimpressive.

Largely for this reason, most antislavery voters during the early 1840s demonstrated an unshakable Whiggishness. To them, Whig economic measures promised to overcome economic parochialism with federal power for the benefit of "free laborers." The states'-rights and laissez-faire programs of the Democrats, on the contrary, stirred images of slaveholding "Nullifiers" busy in the Southern hinterlands opposing projects designed to forward the democratic aspirations of independent farmers, artisans, and professional men everywhere. The same slaveholding interests in the Democratic Party which were already subverting the civil rights of blacks and Northern whites were now depicted as warring with their economic well-being.

The notion that the Whig Party stood for abolition was patently erroneous. Both major parties depended for survival on an intersectional alliance of voters and the slaveholders' goodwill. Yet there was considerable merit to the antislavery Whigs' contentions that using federal power to stimulate free labor was subversive of slaveholders' interests. For one thing, as the Nullification Crisis had demonstrated, many planters now equated the exercise of federal authority over the economy with the possibility of nationally legislated emancipation. Second, antislavery politicians were developing a Whig economic program to expose yet another level of conflict between their own expansive society and the economically "benighted," slavery-retarded South.

Liberty men had always been deeply influenced by these perceptions of Southern economic "backwardness." From the first, abolitionists had entertained glowing visions of a nation wholly redeemed and fruitfully improved by universally free labor. Now, in the early 1840s, it was becoming clear to third-party leaders that their abolitionist arguments were being reinforced by these broader economic themes. By 1842, Joshua Leavitt, Gamaliel Bailey, and especially Salmon P. Chase of Ohio were complaining openly of the crippling effects of the one-idea platform. Hoping to attract new supporters, *The Emancipator* and *The Philanthropist* began featuring editorials which warned of slavery's exploitative influences on Northern laborers.

As early as 1840, Leavitt was admonishing his readers that American economic policy since the election of Jefferson had been "originated by the Slave Power" in order to "make free labor cheap, without lowering the price of cotton." The axiom, endorsed by both major parties, that slave and free labor could prosper "under the same policy" was "just as absurd as perpetual motion, as visionary as the philosopher's stone." Soon Liberty Party journals, convention resolutions, and pamphlets echoed the antislavery Whig appeal: as bloated planter aristocrats fattened their treasuries with the fruits of slave labor, they conspired simultaneously to stifle Northern agriculture, to depress Northern commerce, and to drain off the wages of the Northern workingman. Here, Liberty men believed, were compelling new statements of "truth" which would increase Birney's votes next election day.

A subtle but unmistakable change was overtaking political abolitionism. Moral agitation on behalf of African American equality, the original version of immediate emancipation, was now being subsumed in editorials like Leavitt's by a broader abolitionist fear that slaveholding was subverting the Northern political economy. The Garrisonians' original warnings were proving true. Liberty men were discovering that the rules of political engagement required the subordination of racial egalitarianism within broader ideological appeals. No revolution in moral values was necessary to oppose the "slave power" on the basis of its economic or political threats to "Northern rights"; such opposition, in fact, required little sympathy for slaves in the South and even less for free blacks in the North, a fact that African American abolitionists sensed from the first. It would be a terrible error, warned black Liberty man Samuel Ringgold Ward, "to yield up, compromise, or hold in abeyance any of our . . . vital principles for the sake of making it easier for others to unite with us."

To be sure, individual Liberty men such as Birney, Leavitt, Gerrit Smith, William Goodell, and Lewis Tappan continued steadfast to their deep commitment to black emancipation and race equality. Liberty Party conventions continued to pass resolutions that condemned discrimination in the North as well as Southern enslavement and even nominated African American candidates for office. Even leading antislavery Whigs and Democrats, while hardly consistent egalitarians, often held to views which also were far in advance of the majority's racist norms. The initial idealism of immediatist abolitionism on matters of race was never wholly absent from antislavery politics. Yet embedded in this sensitivity to "Northern rights" were also the makings of a white supremacist's antislavery, a powerful ideology in which racism and sectionalism easily reinforced each other.

Judged in this context, the Garrisonians' hopelessly utopian emphasis on transforming the racial opinions of all white people, not manipulating their voting habits, seems disconcertingly well informed. Still, it seemed just as impossible to abolitionists as it seems to us today to imagine emancipation except by federal government action of some sort. Practicality dictated that all abolitionists, Liberty men and Garrisonians alike, develop positive responses to the onset of sectional politics. By the early 1840s, abolitionists of all persuasions had begun to discover sophisticated political strategies that consciously influenced anti-Southern feeling as it spread in the two major parties. Liberty Party leaders hit upon the technique of supporting in private the same antislavery politicians that they opposed so bitterly in public. From the moment that he replaced Birney as editor of *The Philanthropist*, Gamaliel Bailey offered one rebuke after another to these dissident congressmen. Meanwhile, he was writing personally to Adams, Slade, Gates, and the others, imploring them to make antislavery speeches in defiance of the gag rule. "Abolitionists will help you," he assured them. "What we all wish is *action now.*" Then, late in 1841, Joshua Leavitt, now Washington reporter for *The Emancipator*, privately encouraged the antislavery Whigs to organize as a formal faction, a "select committee" on antislavery, as Giddings liked to call it. Later, Leavitt would join this group as it convened in John Quincy Adams's sitting room. Early in 1842, Theodore D. Weld also joined, serving as a research aide to the antislavery congressmen who, as Leavitt wrote, were now "thoroughly aroused" and ready to agitate on a "whole field" of subjects.

Thanks in part to political abolitionists like Leavitt, Whig leaders found themselves incapable of suppressing the party's antislavery wing. Their attempt to censure Adams for presenting antislavery petitions resulted in an eleven-day "trial" in which the former President mounted as his defense one disquisition after another on the perniciousness of the "slave power." When Adams was "acquitted" on a purely sectional vote, Whigs and Democrats tried to reestablish party discipline by voting to censure the less influential Giddings. Giddings had provided a suitable occasion, for he had offered resolutions affirming the right of slaves to rise in violent mutiny when being shipped in the coastwise slave trade. Resigning his seat,

Giddings was overwhelmingly reelected by his Western Reserve constituents. Liberty men, in this instance, dropped their opposition and voted for him en masse.

By 1842, non-voting Garrisonians had also evolved some surprisingly well-conceived stratagems to interject their radicalism into sectional politics. In contrast to the Liberty Party, they aimed to influence politics without compromising their independence from "corrupted" structures of governance. To this end, Garrison, Wendell Phillips, and many of their associates concentrated on agitation among the constituencies of antislavery politicians while they mercilessly criticized the politicians themselves. When politicians did serve the abolitionist cause, however, Garrisonians were quick to offer support.

For example, when Giddings had been censured and was standing for reelection, Garrison urged that he "be returned by an overwhelming (it ought to be unanimous) vote." Agents of the American Anti-Slavery Society then rushed to his district, hoping to rouse the voters by preaching anti-government doctrines. Edmund Quincy explained this aspect of Garrisonian tactics well, asserting that the best way to encourage antislavery malcontents in the major parties was to preach radicalism to their electors, aiming thereby to make "their conscience(s) uncomfortable." "In nine out of ten cases," he observed, people thus affected would allay their guilt by casting ballots for antislavery candidates. Garrisonians thus remained unfettered by political ties and enjoyed the widest possible freedom to influence sectional politicians in all parties. Even as racism became increasingly compatible with antislavery politics, Garrisonians continued to succeed in thrusting before the voters the uncompromised ideal of black emancipation.

The Garrisonians' political tactics also served other important ends. By demanding "No Union with Slaveholders," Garrisonians lessened a polemical advantage in sectional disagreements enjoyed by states'-rights Southerners. In nearly all circles outside radical abolitionism, Northern responses to the slaveholders' secession threats had smacked of cautious legalism, as congressmen solemnly affirmed the perpetuity of the Union. Garrisonians hoped to correct this imbalance in the sectional debate by reminding Northern politicians that constitutional literalism was no substitute for answering Southern extremism in kind. As Quincy put it tersely in 1847: "Calhoun in the South and Garrison in the North stand front to front . . . Every man must needs be on one side or the other."

Whatever their approaches to politics, abolitionists all agreed that slavery questions bore heavily on the 1844 Presidential election. Since 1840, antislavery feeling had been stimulated by the gag-rule struggles, by several spectacular slave mutinies on the high seas, and by increased reluctance in the North to enforce the 1793 Fugitive Slave Law. In 1842 the Supreme Court ruled in *Prigg v. Pennsylvania* that the power to legislate the return of fugitives lay exclusively with Congress. New Hampshire, Connecticut, Rhode Island, Pennsylvania, Vermont, and Massachusetts consequently enacted "personal liberty laws," denying federal authorities any state assistance in recapturing slaves. Of little practical value to the escapees, these laws nonetheless testified to the continued resentment of Northerners to slaveowning interference in their local affairs. Thus, it is hardly surprising that large numbers of voters balked at the renewed prospect of adding to the Union the still-independent slave territory of Texas.

The fate of slaveowning Henry Clay, the Whig nominee for President, is a good example of how the rising sensitivity to "Northern rights" began disrupting national politics. Clay embodied the contradictions of the middle ground. Though he kept many slaves at his fine Kentucky plantation, he was also a leading advocate of colonization and had criticized the worst practices of slaveholding. This earned him a "moderate's" reputation in the North, but to Deep South slaveholders, he was dangerously unreliable. Clay's economic nationalism further undermined his standing in the Deep South. When advocating national banking, high tariffs, and federally sponsored internal improvements, he also supported the free-labor interests of the border South as well as within the North. Joshua Giddings cheered Clay's economic vision, whereas states'-rights planters grew increasingly nervous.

Clay sought to gain the Presidency by suppressing antagonisms between his Northern and Southern supporters. With his probable Democratic opponent, Martin Van Buren, Clay took steps to remove the issue of the annexation of Texas from the election; both men put out ambiguous statements, hoping to end discussion on this question. But the Democrats surprised Clay by casting Van Buren aside and nominating instead the Tennessee slaveholder James K. Polk on an expansionist platform which called for the immediate annexation of Texas. Hoping also to satisfy the North, the party pledged to acquire all of Oregon as well—a region claimed by England which was clearly not hospitable to plantation settlement.

The Democrats were responding to some of the dominant impulses of the 1840s. The boundaries of the United States had remained fixed since 1819. But by the mid-1840s a new spirit of aggressive nationalism proclaimed that America's "manifest destiny" lay in occupying the entire continent. There were many contradictory motives behind this thrust for continental dominion; the land-hunger of pioneers, Eastern desires for Pacific commercial bases, and fears of European encroachment on the West Coast. To many slaveholders, expansion offered the promise of replacing acreage in the older slave states which was being exhausted by overcultivation or converted to free-labor farming. Creating new slave states out of western territories would also enhance the South's political dominance in the Union. While opposed to these goals, many Northerners nevertheless endorsed expansion as the best way to promote the well-being of independent free laborers and republican institutions. Western territories should be distributed at low cost to individual settlers to alleviate compounding problems of urban poverty and to prevent artificial concentrations of agrarian wealth.

In promising to annex Texas and occupy Oregon, the Democrats were attempting to accommodate the conflicting ideals of the slave plantation and the free-labor family farm, a difficult undertaking. Instead of mollifying sectional passions, they would manipulate them for partisan advantage over Henry Clay. This platform also increased the likelihood of war with Mexico, which refused to recognize the independence of its former province. American military success could bring even greater conquests from Mexico, whose boundaries encompassed huge expanses of North American territory.

In the midst of these developments, a much better-organized Liberty Party renominated James G. Birney on a broadly anti-Southern platform which emphasized the "slave power's" sinister role in promoting Texas annexation and undermining "Northern rights." Clay now had to worry about defections in the North as well as in the South as his supporters pressed him to make his position clear on sectional issues. To the discomfort of slaveholders everywhere, Northern spokesmen of both parties emphasized their anti-Southern stance, hoping to minimize the Liberty Party vote. Antislavery Whigs, meantime, issued extravagant claims for Clay, even picturing him as anxious to abolish slavery in the District of Columbia. The candidate's fellow Kentuckian, abolitionist Cassius Clay, campaigned throughout the Midwest on behalf of his namesake.

Embarrassed by his own supporters, Clay could only dissimulate on the Texas question, hoping to keep his coalition together. Significant numbers of antislavery Whig voters responded with increasing disgust at Clay's "slippery tactics." "He is as rotten as a stagnant fishpond on the subject of slavery and always has been," Seth M. Gates declared as he renounced his Whig allegiance and voted for Birney. And it was voters such as Gates, Whigs charged in the election's aftermath, who doomed Clay's campaign. Enough of them in New York State, Whigs contended, had switched from Clay to Birney to deliver that state's thirty-six electoral votes, and the Presidency, to Polk and the "slaveocracy."

Liberty Party abolitionists like Lewis Tappan claimed at the time that they preferred as President "an out and out friend and advocate of slavery" like Polk to "an intriguer" like Clay. Yet the significance of this election lay far less in who got the most votes than in the fact that the political process had begun to foster feelings of sectionalism. For a decade longer, orthodox political loyalties to the two major parties would prove strong enough to withstand these corrosive disagreements. But the 1844 defeat of Henry Clay clearly portended more volatile elections to come in which ambiguity like Clay's would have ever-diminishing import.

While national elections in the 1840s invited white Liberty men to deemphasize their racial egalitarianism, many of their black colleagues were working toward opposite ends. Bridling at their political exclusion and frustrated by mounting conflicts over slavery in which they could not participate as voters, a large number of African American activists, most of them Liberty Party supporters, began as early as 1840 to discuss the possibility of campaigns to secure the franchise. After several more years of debate and preparation, they chose New York as the most likely state for victory. Here, at least, a few wealthy black men were already allowed to vote. New York State politics, moreover, promised these activists significant white allies. The state sustained the Liberty Party's best-established organization and its Whig Party included strongly antislavery leaders like William Seward and Horace Greeley.

Henry Highland Garnet, more than anyone else, imparted

to this movement its focus and momentum. An escapee from Maryland, Garnet represented the new generation of fugitives and free black men which would define African American political activism until the end of the Civil War. Educated at New York City's African Free School and at Beriah Green's Oneida Institute, Garnet had developed friendships with politically minded activists such as Alexander Crummell, James McCune Smith, George T. Downing, and Samuel Ringgold Ward, all of whom now joined him in the New York suffrage effort. The year 1841 saw Garnet addressing the state legislature and presenting the first of many petitions. After five more years of preparation, when a convention was called by the legislature to revise the state constitution, Garnet and his colleagues were ready to press an all-out campaign.

Though the convention did agree to remove the voting restrictions, the statewide referendum that followed brought disaster to Garnet and his allies. White Liberty men remained loyal supporters, but neither of the two major parties proved able to stomach the measure. The Democrats' uniform hostility was expected, but the deep split caused by "equal suffrage" among New York's Whigs had discouraging implications. Instead of stimulating the politics of freedom, the equal-suffrage issue taught the Whigs a not-to-be-forgotten lesson: involving their party in racial reform meant dividing it fatally, thereby forfeiting elections to Democrats.

As Pennsylvania's black Whigs and Liberty men likewise discovered when their equal-suffrage amendment was crushed in 1848, racism among Northern voters was far too deeply embedded to foster a politics of racial equality. Before the Civil War, only the New England states (save Connecticut) among all the Northern states allowed all black men to vote, a situation that certainly seemed to bear out Garrisonian warnings about the corruption of white men's politics. It likewise supported the lament of James McCune Smith, a prominent black

Liberty man, that the electorate harbored "a hate deeper than I had imagined" toward people like himself.

Slave rebels, though unintentionally, sometimes exercised a more potent impact on white men's politics than did Northern activists like Smith and Garnet. The decade of the 1840s was punctuated by several well-publicized slave-ship mutinies which caused antislavery politicians to defend black insurrectionists. The first of these took place on the high seas in 1839 aboard the Spanish vessel *Amistad* when the slaves rose up, killed several crewmen, and attempted to set a course for Africa. After they beached instead on Long Island Sound, Lewis Tappan secured the legal services of John Quincy Adams for them in protracted litigations that finally reached the Supreme Court, which ordered the captives freed and returned to Africa.

As these court battles proceeded amid extraordinary publicity, political figures as diverse as New York Whig leader William Seward, New York Democrat Jabez Hammond, Liberty Party standard-bearer James G. Birney, and Garrisonian Wendell Phillips joined Adams in endorsing the insurrectionists. John C. Calhoun, the Great Nullifier, saw in such responses a disturbing willingness on the part of Northern whites to justify the actions of "a band of murderous slaves with hands stained in blood."

Calhoun soon had even greater reason for worry in the aftermath of another slave-ship uprising, this time in 1841 on the brig *Creole*. This, as we have seen, led to Congressman Joshua Giddings's being censured and expelled from the House of Representatives after presenting resolutions to defend the *Creole* slaves' right to revolt. When the voters in a special election overwhelmingly returned him to his seat, it was with specific instructions that he offer his "insurrectionist" resolutions once again. When he did so, and when nearly all his Northern Whig colleagues supported him, Calhoun was right to wonder how much of Giddings's support was due to simple partisanship and how much actually reflected the congressmen's willingness to countenance slave violence. While largely hostile to black equality, some Yankee politicians and the white men who elected them proved surprisingly responsive to violent rebellion by slaves. The feelings aroused by the *Creole* and *Amistad* uprisings in the 1840s foreshadowed the militant spirit that would surround John Brown in the following decade.

Mid-1846 witnessed militancy of a wholly different sort after Texas was finally annexed and President Polk opened hostilities against Mexico. Antislavery feeling in Northern politics suddenly spread with unprecedented speed as opposition to the "slave power's" further expansion deepened among abolitionists of all sorts, within New England's intelligentsia and, most significantly, in the minds of some well-established Whig and Democratic politicians. Garrisonians took satisfaction in trumpeting that the war proved once again what they had known all along — that all political parties and governmental instruments, like all American institutions, were hopelessly corrupted by slaveowning: "The motto enscribed on the banner of Freedom should be NO UNION WITH SLAVEHOLDERS!" Though few took Garrison's advice literally, as events in the Mexican War years built toward a sectional confrontation, Northern politicians in increasing numbers came to conclusions roughly similar to his about the limits of their loyalty to the Union.

In 1846, Wendell Phillips noted these trends approvingly, writing that Northerners who once "would have whispered Disunion with white lips now love to talk about it." Many "leading men," he predicted, "will soon talk as we were once laughed at for talking . . ." Phillips, in fact, was understating matters. Even before the 1844 elections, twelve Northern congressmen, led by Adams, Gates, and Giddings, issued a public warning that if Texas was annexed as a slave state the Union would no longer have a moral basis to retain the loyalty of citizens in the North. In 1845 the Massachusetts and Ohio legislatures threatened to refuse to comply with the federal statutes which enabled Texas statehood. In 1846 Giddings himself treated all politicians to the bewildering spectacle of running successfully for reelection while denying the moral authority of the government in which he sought to retain his place.

To be sure, Garrisonian disunion was inextricably linked with immediate emancipation, whereas these "disunionist politicians" objected primarily to adding new slave states. Yet William Jay, a most perceptive abolitionist, sensed correctly that these espousals of disunion reflected a common "state of mind." As Southern demands intensified, greater numbers of Northerners were willing, like the Garrisonians, to question the nation's fundamental assumptions and some of their own unionist attachments. Could a truly republican government be equally dedicated to the contradictory interests of aristocratic slaveholders and self-sufficient free laborers? Must federal power involve Northern citizens in retrieving the planters' slaves? Must Northern voters be called on, time and again, to endorse and then underwrite programs which promoted the expansion of slavery? Or should "freedom-loving Northerners" rethink the meaning of union and discard their loyalty to a system dominated by "slave power"?

In religion as well as in politics, the severing of one's attachments to pro-slavery institutions became an excellent measure of mounting personal alienation and sectional pressures. Stephen S. Foster and Parker Pillsbury practiced the doctrine during the 1840s in garish forms of which most other Garrisonians disapproved, disrupting church services in New England with uninvited lectures on organized religion's complicity with the sin of slavery. Often the parishioners would force them bodily to the door. More often, abolitionists like Gerrit Smith and Lewis Tappan withdrew from their denominations to found independent "free" churches in which slavery was recognized as a sin. Thus, Presbyterians, Baptists, and Congregationalists all experienced serious defections in the East and the Northwest, and among the Methodists in 1845 a formal division took place between pro-slavery and antislavery wings.

Repelled by the clergy's stubborn resistance to immediatism, and the hollow sacramentalism of conventional worship, other abolitionists sought spontaneous, intensely personal religious experiences which led to no denominational upheavals. Abolitionists like Theodore D. Weld, Angelina Grimké Weld, Lydia Maria Child, Elizur Wright, Jr., and many others moved toward a diffuse, disorganized "religion of humanity," hoping, as one explained, to be "less orthodox but more Christian" by scrapping formal theology for a pure humanitarian creed. For some seekers, the quest led still further, to espousals of religious anarchism and efforts to build holy communities of religious perfectionists and utopian socialists wherein no discordant human enactments could interrupt the harmony of Divine Law. Beyond even this, as Elizur Wright, Jr., discovered, was atheism, the doctrine he embraced at the end of his lifelong pilgrimage.

But it was antislavery rebels in the two major parties, not spiritually restless abolitionists, who most powerfully destabilized the political order during the Mexican War years. Among the Whigs, old insurgents like John Quincy Adams now found support from aggressive and much younger men. Old Man Eloquent's son, Charles Francis Adams, was prominent among them. Ever since 1845, established anti-sectional Whig leaders from Massachusetts, men like Robert Winthrop and Daniel Webster, had found themselves confronted by noisy antislavery opponents, "Conscience Whigs" as they called themselves. Among the latter were men destined for careers as the North's foremost sectional politicians—Charles Sumner, Henry Wilson, and the younger Adams. By 1847, these men were deep in correspondence with Whig dissidents in other states and also with significant antislavery elements which had now begun to group within the Northern Democrats. Both segments in turn began discussing strategy with Gamaliel Bailey, Joshua Leavitt, Salmon P. Chase, and other Liberty Party leaders.

Among the Northern Democrats, a rising hostility toward their party's policy of expanding slavery was reinforced by deep political resentment against James K. Polk. Especially in New York, Martin Van Buren and his supporters began voicing concern that their party was rapidly being overrun by the "slave power's" influence. The party's future in the North (and theirs) depended on maintaining the traditional policy of supporting slavery generally while suppressing sectional discord, Van Burenites felt. But, from the start, Polk's policies seemed to run in an opposite, exclusively pro-slavery direction. Van Buren supporters in Ohio, Massachusetts, and Pennsylvania, as well as in New York, were ever more concerned that their party was becoming unacceptable to Northern voters. Polk's unwillingness to satisfy the Van Buren Democrats' patronage expectations, his vetoes of bills to subsidize river and harbor improvements, and his failure to annex all of Oregon seemed in retrospect new signs of the "slave power's" increasing domination of the party.

Most ominous of all was the growth of these feelings in the Van Burenites' constituencies as Whig and Liberty Party opponents began to lure away voters with antislavery appeals. Hoping to arrest the "slave power's" momentum, a group of Northern Democratic representatives introduced in Congress in August 1846 the instantly famous Wilmot Proviso. Named after Pennsylvania congressman David Wilmot, the Proviso, which was not to pass both houses of Congress before the Civil War, stipulated that slavery be excluded from all territory acquired through war with Mexico.

The demand for "free soil" — for territory in which slavery would be prohibited forever — had now been thrust into the center of American politics. From then on, all agreed that the nation's future depended on whether slaveholding planters or "republican free laborers" shaped the development of this vast region. In the early 1830s a tiny abolitionist minority had asked for "immediate emancipation." By the early 1840s, Liberty men and antislavery Whigs had broadened the antislavery appeal to express concerns for civil liberties and the economic dimensions of "Northern rights." Now, with the Wilmot Proviso, the antislavery movement was expanding further still, emphasizing the primacy of free soil, the curtailing of "slave power," and the imperative to secure Northern supremacy within the Union. This was an ideology capable of uniting powerful and otherwise antagonistic interests into a common anti-Southern front; but in it the abolitionist commitment to black equality could expect little, if any, recognition.

Liberty men, well aware of these facts, grew increasingly divided as the 1848 Presidential election neared. Veterans like James G. Birney, Joshua Leavitt, and Gerrit Smith recalled with disgust Martin Van Buren's strident anti-abolitionism during the 1830s. The unabashed willingness of Van Burenites to support vast territorial conquests from unoffending Mexico in the name of free soil also filled them with misgivings. So did clarifying statements like the one David Wilmot offered in 1846: "I would preserve for free white labor a fair country, a rich inheritance, where the sons of toil, of my own race and color, can live without the disgrace which association with negro slavery brings upon free labor."

Other members of the party, led by Gamaliel Bailey, Henry B. Stanton, and Salmon P. Chase, stressed political "realism" and urged coalition with antislavery Whigs and Democrats. Birney, though already renominated, should step aside in favor of John P. Hale, a national figure whose Democratic background might appeal to Van Burenites. Meanwhile, Whigs like Charles Francis Adams pressed hard for the antislavery Democrats and Liberty men to unite behind any number of "Northern rights" candidates. As Garrisonians kept up a drumfire of reminders that support of free soil meant capitulation to "white man's antislavery," political abolitionists everywhere faced an agonizing decision: where did "realism" lie. Was it found in compromise, in joining the largest antislavery groundswell to date and then trying to improve its racist tone? If so, the Garrisonians had a point; pitfalls of expedience lay ahead. Or did "realism" mean holding on to principle, adhering to the doctrines of immediate emancipation and black equality? If so, then the Liberty Party most certainly would appear, as it had to so many in 1840, as a cranky sect, removed from even the periphery of significant political activity.

In August 1848, Liberty Party abolitionists had to choose. The Whig and Democratic leaders, still trying to suppress sectional tensions, had ratified their platforms and selected their candidates. The results guaranteed the defection of the Van Buren Democrats and the antislavery Whigs. Lewis Cass of Michigan, an old 1812 War hero, received the Democratic nomination on a platform of "popular sovereignty," which meant transferring from Congress to the people of each territory the responsibility of deciding whether or not to adopt slavery. The Whigs, by contrast, decided that the best approach to slavery questions was silence; they adopted no platform at all and nominated a politically inexperienced slaveholding general, Zachary Taylor. Voters in antislavery districts clamored for third-party revolt and were ready, as one local correspondent put it, to "pronounce a valedictory on the dead and rotten carcass[es]" of the two national parties. Van Buren Democrats, Conscience Whigs, and Liberty Party leaders thereupon held a Presidential convention of their own in Buffalo.

The Free-Soil Party, as the new party called itself, conjoined such diverse political types as the great fugitive-orator Frederick Douglass, Liberty man Joshua Leavitt, and former President Van Buren. After much political dealing, the abolitionists' old antagonist, Van Buren, accepted the Free-Soil Party nomination; to satisfy antislavery Whigs, the convention chose Charles Francis Adams as Van Buren's running mate. The platform, far more limited in its antislavery stance than any the Liberty Party had ever presented, endorsed the Proviso with the slogan "Free Soil, Free Speech, Free Labor, Free Men" and declared that the federal government must "relieve itself of all [constitutional] responsibility for the existence and continuance of slavery." The rest of the platform dealt with those broad economic issues which had for some time been increasingly intertwined with antislavery, particularly homestead laws and federally sponsored internal improvements. Liberty men could not help but notice the omission of any pledge to assist free blacks or to work for immediate emancipation. Their time of decision was at hand: whether to join these dissident Whigs and Democrats or to depart from the convention, doctrines intact.

Most chose to stay. Joshua Leavitt in a moving speech urged Liberty Party delegates to believe that their party was simply being "translated" into something larger and more effective without serious loss of principle. Many other political abolitionists with impeccable credentials agreed, campaigned for Van Buren, and imparted to the Free-Soil cause a higher egalitarian tone than it might otherwise have had. Other white Liberty men like Gerrit Smith and William Goodell, as well as black colleagues like Henry Highland Garnet, could not accept the Free-Soil Party's limited doctrines and "tainted" candidates. Leaving the proceedings in protest, they endorsed legislated emancipation and organized themselves as the Liberty League, a splinter group that attracted the support of several prominent black activists. As a fourth party, they functioned until 1861 much as the non-voting Garrisonians did, prodding antislavery politicians and insisting on a redeemed America, free of racism and slavery.

During the same hot July that saw dissident politicians organizing the Free-Soil Party in Buffalo, abolitionist women convened in nearby Seneca Falls to establish the nation's first women's-rights movement. It was more than coincidence that the two events overlapped as they did; the same dynamics that inspired antislavery politics were not proving beneficial to abolitionist feminists, so Elizabeth Cady Stanton traveled to Seneca Falls, while her husband, Henry, a fervid "Liberty man," joined the Free-Soilers in Buffalo. To Cady Stanton and her associates, the time had arrived for independent action on behalf of women's rights.

After the abolitionist movement had shattered in 1840, the level of female activism within the cause as a whole quickly declined. Many of the local female antislavery societies collapsed or sustained themselves largely with routine activities and social events. In the face of mounting political discussion by Liberty men and Free-Soilers, petitioning women generally resumed the conventions of the "women's sphere," deferentially signing their names Mrs. or Miss. The issues they addressed involved benevolence and charity, matters close to family and church, far removed from earlier contests over emancipation and equal rights.

Leadership opportunities for women within the antislavery societies also diminished. The vote-driven Liberty Party of necessity excluded women from its councils, and among the evangelical abolitionists who rallied around Lewis Tappan, male dominance prevailed. Only within the American Anti-Slavery Society, where powerful men like Wendell Phillips, Edmund Quincy, and William Lloyd Garrison stood foursquare in favor of women's rights, could female abolitionists exercise power and responsibility. Thus, women's-rights luminaries such as

Abby Kelley Foster, Lucretia Mott, Sara Pugh, and Elizabeth Cady Stanton all drew their initial motivation from their labors as Garrisonians. But even here it was clear that women's rights necessarily had a lower priority; the American Anti-Slavery Society placed a greater premium on agitating for disunion than on promoting women's rights.

The Seneca Falls Convention sought to reverse these priorities with resolutions that objected to the lack of educational and professional opportunities for women and that demanded equal control by wives over family property and over children in cases of divorce. After calling for the "overthrow of the monopoly of the pulpit" and for "equal participation with men in the various trades, professions and commerce," the convention presented one additional resolution that proved so controversial that it alone failed to pass unanimously. It stated that women must fight "to gain the sacred right of the elective franchise." Garrisonian women who condemned men for voting in a "corrupted" political system saw no inconsistency in demanding the vote for themselves. If voting ever became a morally responsible action, they reasoned, it certainly should not be restricted to men, an argument transferred wholesale from their Garrisonian backgrounds.

The tie between the Garrisonians and the women's-rights movement continued to be close. Seneca Falls prompted the formation of local women's-rights groups and inspired regional gatherings in Salem, Ohio (where men were barred from speaking), and in Worcester, Massachusetts. But the association with Garrisonianism brought problems as well as benefits. Problems took the form of implicit tensions between the Garrisonian dream of a "moral revolution" that offered "equal suffrage" for both races and genders and the far more feasible possibility of equal citizenship for white women alone. These divided loyalties to broad-based racial equality and to their own self-interest would finally burst forth among feminists at the end of the Civil War, when debates began in earnest over granting voting rights exclusively to emancipated male slaves. The bonds between feminism and radical abolitionism also proved of incontestable value. Garrisonians, for one thing, supplied the new movement with some extraordinary male supporters who offered substantial rebuttals to warnings that behind women's rights lurked the threat of female dictatorship. For another, Garrison's *Liberator* and similar publications provided widely circulating vehicles for feminist writers and speakers that no independent women's-rights journal such as Pauline Davis's *Una* could ever equal. In addition, there can be little doubt that each cause endowed the other with a powerful new motivation, since "the slavery of sex" and sexual exploitation inherent in Southern slavery seemed to these reformers so disturbingly intertwined.

Finally, and most important for the politics of the sectional conflict, the rise of women's rights inspired a powerful new visceral revulsion among planters against all that Yankee culture embodied. Wedded to ancient values of honor which celebrated their dominion over their many "dependents," slaveholders reacted with understandable anger to all perceived transgressions of hearth and home. For better than a decade, as they saw it, Yankee fanatics had attacked them personally as fathers, husbands, and men when condemning their just rule over their slaves. By embracing women's rights, these zealots were now attempting to engineer the feminizing of manhood, the overthrow of masculinity itself. Look at effeminate Wendell Phillips, one Southern editorialist exclaimed. "Perhaps if a civil war should come," he jeered, "Mr. Phillips would be surrounded by a life-guard of elderly maidens, protected by a rampart of whale-bone and cotton wadding." The sexual contents of sectional politics were never far from the surface as disagreements multiplied between North and South. The women's movement, more than any other agent, made these deeper conflicts ever more explicit and the politics of slavery all the more volatile.

To a much greater extent than in 1844, the 1848 elections emphasized volatility. Northern politicians in the two major parties now outdid one another in their antislavery stances, seeking to minimize losses to the Free-Soilers. Southern Whigs and Democrats again worried that abolitionism was overtaking the Northern wings of their parties. Supporters of the third party in turn mounted a sophisticated campaign, and as in 1844, third-party voting patterns in New York seem to have decided the Presidential outcome, this time in favor of the Whigs. Although it captured no electoral votes, the Free-Soil Party did win in twelve congressional races. Where its nominees were defeated, it was often by major-party candidates like Pennsylvania's Thaddeus Stevens, a Whig with unshakable antislavery convictions.

This newly elected Congress, so highly charged with North–South antagonisms, had to decide what to do with the lands taken from Mexico. Many slaveholders, alarmed by continuing emancipation in South America, expressed increasing concern that the South was being encircled by free territory. The South needed to expand westward, to secure new territory against the forces of worldwide abolitionism. Slaveholders also expected to employ slave labor in the mines of New Mexico and California and in plantation agriculture in the Colorado, Rio Grande, and Gila river valleys. Besides, soil exhaustion and surplus slaves, the political realities of sectional balance, and the promise of huge profits had driven the slaveholding states to double their area since 1800. As abolitionists watched from the sidelines, bipartisan politicians in Congress struggled to reconcile the contradictory demands of sectional expansion and national unity.

The result, as in 1820, was compromise, arranged by politicians who again separated the question of slavery's morality from the political process. Abolitionists everywhere joined in a rising chorus of disgust as Daniel Webster, Henry Clay, and especially Stephen A. Douglas of Illinois sponsored a series of measures designed to preserve the political balance between the sections and to bury disputes over slavery forever. "What a travesty on the mathematics of justice," Garrison exclaimed, "to announce excitedly that two and two make six, to argue a bit about it, and then to shake hands on the number five!" Congress voted to admit California to the Union as a free state, and slaveholding Texas, already a state, was awarded ten million dollars for giving up its extensive territorial claims in New Mexico. In New Mexico and Utah, new territories, the slavery-extension question was to be solved later by popular sovereignty, which aimed to place the decision in the hands of the settlers themselves. As a concession to the North, slave-trading (but not the practice of holding slaves) was prohibited in the District of Columbia. To right the balance, Congress amended the 1793 Fugitive Slave Law to include new, far harsher provisions. The law authorized federal commissioners, not state judges, to process fugitives, and every Northern citizen was obliged to assist in the capture of escapees. Whites who abetted the escape of slaves now risked severe penalties, and the fugitives themselves were deprived of the right to trial by jury or the opportunity to testify. Free blacks found themselves in jeopardy of being summarily claimed as escaped slaves, seized, and shipped south.

Slaveowners saw in this law a sweeping assertion of their power within the Union. The abolitionists agreed. So flagrant was its violation of judicial procedure that many Northerners otherwise not hostile to slavery joined in opposing it. The gag rule and the anti-abolitionist violence of the 1830s and 1840s and the Fugitive Slave Law of the 1850s served to fuse anti-slavery feeling with an increasingly pervasive fear of the "slave power's" dominion. Most of all, the Fugitive Slave Law reminded apathetic whites, through the resistance it provoked, that militant black men and women were struggling in all regions to secure freedom and justice for their race. Henry Clay was fond of repeating, in the aftermath of the Compromise of 1850, that permanent peace now prevailed "throughout all of our borders." At the same time, black abolitionists, white sympathizers, and the slaves themselves began committing acts which destroyed Clay's vision of permanent domestic tranquillity.

6

RACES, CLASSES, AND FREEDOM

In October 1851, Jerry McHenry, a free black resident of Syracuse, New York, was seized by federal marshals acting under the Fugitive Slave Law. Six hours later he found himself on the road to Canada, liberated by a crowd of indignant African Americans and whites who had successfully stormed his jail cell. Gerrit Smith and Samuel J. May had contrived Jerry McHenry's rescue with black abolitionists Samuel Ringgold Ward and Jermain Loguen. Subsequently, twenty-six individuals were indicted for violating the law — twelve black, fourteen white.

Incidents even more dramatic than the Jerry McHenry rescue in Syracuse were to punctuate the 1850s, promoting militant interracial collaboration against the new Fugitive Slave Law. Long before this decade of resistance to "slave catchers," however, abolitionists of both races had fully tested the limits of interracial collaboration. Cooperation, black and white reformers discovered, was often natural, inevitable, and immensely beneficial. Yet, as often as not, African Americans and whites found themselves working at cross-purposes, divided not only by racial antagonisms common within American cultures but also by attitudes peculiar to abolitionism itself.

Inspired by religious fervor that fostered their hatred of "sin," white abolitionists sensed a total antithesis between the concepts of slavery and freedom: the one was evil incarnate, the other partook of God's perfect grace. For whites, moreover, enslavement and emancipation paralleled other moral opposites — guilt and innocence, damnation and salvation, sublimation and self-liberation. This value system, based on fixed abstractions, allowed white abolitionists to empathize far more deeply than any previous group of whites with the trials endured by the enslaved. But it also made it difficult for whites to fathom what so many black activists understood by the term "freedom."

Drawing on lifetimes of discrimination, Northern blacks were painfully aware that complete freedom and formal enslavement represented extremes. Between them lay complicated circumstances that allowed for more freedom or less, for more discrimination or less, for a more or less intense sense of enslavement. To be sure, this enslavement involved no specific master. Yet the circumstances facing Northern blacks made their sense of enslavement far more vivid and personal than whites could fully appreciate. The difficulties of surviving left no room for Northern African Americans to dwell on abstract moral categories so familiar to white abolitionists.

Never having felt caste oppression, some white abolitionists understandably found it difficult to grasp the fact that, through exclusion from juries, elections, decent schools, and gainful employment, Northern blacks continuously grappled with a white world that treated them with scorn. For African Americans, far more than for whites, bondage in the South and discrimination in the North constituted two aspects of the single national problem of white supremacy. Their day-to-day actions to counter prejudice in the North therefore took on a pragmatism and complexity which most white reformers could not wholly understand.

The white reformers' cultural ethos and successful class position added to racial division. The sincere egalitarian professions of men like Wendell Phillips, the Tappan brothers, and William Lloyd Garrison must be placed in the context of a Northern white Protestantism incapable of developing what in a later age would be called a multicultural perspective. White abolitionists placed high premium on achieving a society governed by uniform moral codes and systems of ethics that applied to all people regardless of race, gender, religious preference, or economic status. Provincial elites such as slaveholders and "gentlemen of property and standing," as well as pockets of ethnicity and poverty — the poor Southern whites, the English urban poor, and the Irish immigrants — all aroused the abolitionists' deepest suspicions and their impulses to preach of "a better way."

Given these predispositions, their generally secure social position, enormous bureaucratic skills, and belief in the power of conversion, it would be surprising indeed if even the most sympathetic white abolitionists had not attempted to make over the lives of African Americans. It was natural for most white reformers to assume that black culture had little to recommend it and that blacks needed benevolent guidance to work hard, embrace piety, and avoid vice.

Most Northern black leaders expressed strong concurrence with the whites' stern moral designs. Whites looked on approvingly as black activists worked tirelessly throughout the North, establishing Bible societies, moral-reform associations, and other benevolent projects which seemed to replicate white organizations. Yet such movements sprang from complex motives which often misled whites and which were hardly tantamount to "selling out the race." Indeed, in the process of accommodation could be found the seeds of further estrangement and misunderstanding. White responses to black efforts in temperance reform provide a clear illustration of the point.

In temperance, African American leaders found a national cause, universally popular with white abolitionists, and rich in personal meaning and community promise. By the 1840s, blacks had formed statewide temperance societies in Connecticut and New York, as well as an additional organization which embraced these two states and Massachusetts. Every major Northern city had similar organizations, and so did many smaller towns. In Cincinnati, fully one-quarter of the black population had "taken the pledge," avowing that in abstinence from alcohol lay the surest path to honesty, modesty, thrift, and Christian rectitude. "If there is any people who have a good reason for advocating the passage of some kind of prohibatory liquor law," declared one African American enthusiast, "it is the Colored people of this country." White evangelicals such as Lewis Tappan or Gerrit Smith could not have felt more warmly benevolent toward "noble sentiments" such as these.

These black espousals of Protestant values reflected no desire to curry favor with pious white philanthropists and certainly no belief that drunkenness was a burden peculiar to African American culture. African American temperance leaders acted out of race pride, challenging the community to gather its resources, to demonstrate its vitality, and to channel its capital from personal consumption to income-producing enterprise. Too often, however, white abolitionists mistakenly saw in these activities only cheering evidence that "moral uplift" was proceeding apace. Their paternalism became only more burdensome to black activists, who soon found themselves forced to defend their autonomy from overbearing white associates. "It is nothing but this moral elevation that causes us to have so little confidence in one another," black abolitionist Peter Paul Simons exclaimed. "It is this alone that puts white men even at the head of our private affairs . . . This moral elevation is but a mere song, a conspicuous scarecrow designed expressly to hinder our people from acting collectively for ourselves."

As Simons and other African American abolitionists knew, behind the pressures of paternalism could lie more destructive forms of prejudice. As the ranks of the lower classes swelled with immigrants and as cities grew rapidly in size and complexity, insecure Northern whites in every walk of life embraced racist doctrines with accelerated intensity. When white abolitionists committed themselves to oppose all prejudice, they were taking on a far more daunting task than they could possibly have foreseen, and it is certainly not surprising that white abolitionists proved unable to discern the extent of their own biases. Even in the language of unprejudiced white abolitionists like Wendell Phillips, echoes of unconscious white superiority could be detected.

Phillips's aristocratic temperament led him to belittle practically anybody, from Daniel Webster on down. On this ground, his derision of a black associate's clothing must be dismissed; he did the same to seedily dressed white colleagues. Moreover, his devotion to Garrisonian strategies, not racism, was what led him to denigrate African American activists like Frederick Douglass and James W. C. Pennington, who both became supporters of the Liberty Party; Phillips assumed the worst about all Liberty Party leaders. But whenever he found himself riding on a segregated railway, he always protested by sitting in the "negro coach." On a personal level, black associates found him generous and dependable, someone who understood their problems and respected their points of view. Wholly secure in his sense of his personal identity, Phillips was incontestably one of the most racially democratic people of his age.

However, in his much-acclaimed speeches, so compelling in content, so beautifully delivered, so enormously popular, lay themes which emphasized the almost mystical Anglo-Saxon nature of America's heroic history and destiny, which celebrated the Teutonic–Puritan sources of American democracy. In 1859, for example, Phillips called for bold action against the South and spoke for the exercise of "an element in Yankee blood, an impulsive, enthusiastic aspiration, something left to us from the old Puritan stock." It was this essence, he believed, "which made England what she was two centuries ago" and which would sustain the North in "the closest grapple with the Slave Power today." Redemption of the South would "come from the interference of [this] wiser, higher, more advanced civilization" which had first "crept around our shores" from England in the seventeenth century.

Here was an evocation of Anglo-Saxon power which was clearly not racist but which some who heard Phillips might nonetheless apply in a white supremacist manner. Theodore Parker, for example, developed most of his militant abolitionism on the assumption that emancipation of the inferior black race would usher in a glorious new era where Anglo-Saxon values would enjoy complete dominance. This historical racism suffused the thinking of whites of all classes and regions, even circulating to some extent within abolitionism as well. Hence, as they tried to manage antislavery societies, start newspapers, and develop projects of rebellion, African American abolitionists could easily find themselves estranged from their white colleagues by the distinctions of race, culture, and class.

Initial appreciation of the white immediatists for attacking colonization soon diminished among African American abolitionists as they began to notice how underrepresented they were in the antislavery societies. Discomfort heightened in the later 1830s as Liberty men involved themselves in white civil-liberties issues while white Garrisonians expounded on women's rights and religious perfectionism. Both groups, distracted, now protested less often about racial inequality in the North. *The Colored American*, edited by Samuel D. Cornish, hotly asserted that these new questions were "*neither parts nor parcels*" of the struggle for black freedom. In 1843, Frederick Douglass and another talented African American orator, Charles L. Remond, clashed openly with white Garrisonian John A. Collins, denying Collins's contention that his espousals of Christian socialism should supersede discussions of slave emancipation at antislavery gatherings. Nor was this debate purely ideological. The Boston bluestocking Maria Weston Chapman, along with other white Garrisonians, paternalistically "forgave" Douglass and Remond their anger, dismissing their dissent as reflecting a lack of intellectual sophistication and disadvantaged backgrounds.

It is easy to cite other incidents which illustrate the limits of some white immediatists' commitments to racial equality. Garrison's denunciations of Frederick Douglass for endorsing the Liberty Party and starting his own newspaper is only one of the most well known. Insisting that there was "a roguery somewhere," Garrison characterized Douglass's independent decisions as "destitute of every principle of honor, ungrateful to the last degree, and malevolent in spirit." Another oft-cited instance of white abolitionist racism is Arthur Tappan's consistent failure to hire blacks for responsible positions in his mercantile business.

On more subtle levels of gender identity, some white abolitionists also found the limits of their racial egalitarianism. For pious whites, female and male alike, immediatism provided a means to express transformed understandings of themselves as men and women. For white women like Angelina Grimké and Abby Kelley Foster, opposition to Southern slavery highlighted a growing personal sense of sexual enslavement by the conventions of male supremacy that led them directly to women's rights. White men like Wendell Phillips and Thomas Wentworth Higginson found in immediatism a medium for expressing a yearning for masculine heroism that supported their public displays of militant leadership. In all such formulations, images of African Americans served as powerful imaginative vehicles that satisfied the deeper needs of white reformers, a fact that accounts for the widespread presence of self-abasing "Uncle Toms," supplicating bondspeople, and doomed "tragic mulattoes" in white abolitionist writings.

Still, in this analysis, a more important factor must be stressed. Genuine interracial understanding has been rare in the United States, accomplished by only the most discerning of both races, and individuals blessed with such insights were richly represented in the abolitionist movement. One can never know whether discomfort or respectful understanding was more often the result of Weld's or Garrison's habit, when traveling, of boarding in the homes of black abolitionists. One can only imagine what black and white undergraduates at Oberlin discovered about themselves and one another during their years together in college. What is certain is that it gains little to blame the abolitionists because of their prejudices for America's continuing race problems. Hampered in their time by biases rooted in culture, class, and perception of the meaning of "race," many abolitionists, African American and white alike, nevertheless explored the furthest possible boundaries of egalitarianism imaginable in their age. That their efforts led as often to frustration as to mutual understanding should hardly be surprising. That they also worked together so often and so well, and aired their differences so honestly, remains a tribute to their patience, persistence, and wisdom.

Most often, black abolitionists put their frustrations with white colleagues to constructive purpose. By the 1830s, they had established institutions and programs in which they, not whites, determined policy and which served the ends of freedom as the African American community understood them. One of the earliest manifestations of this trend was the National Negro Convention Movement, launched in 1830 and destined to experience periods of relapse and resurgence into the twentieth century. The antebellum history of this enterprise gives some insight into the evolving nature of black abolitionism.

The first National Conventions, which gathered from 1830 to 1835, were dominated by wealthy free African Americans, high-ranking black clergymen, and white philanthropists. James Forten, an affluent black sailmaker, supported the early conventions, as did Bishop Richard Allen, a founder of the African Methodist Episcopal Church. The conventions' deliberations condemned slavery, of course, but put greatest emphasis on conditions in the North, stressing self-help and protesting discrimination. The elite delegates made little headway, however, in establishing local conventions which could support their appeals. From 1835 to 1843, the National Convention failed to assemble, for its African American leaders were temporarily caught up in the white immediatist cause.

By 1843, however, the movement was in full revival, staffed by new leaders and supported by a wide network of auxiliaries. In the eight-year hiatus, black activists had discovered their underrepresentation in white abolitionism and had seen their goals and those of the American Anti-Slavery Society evolving in different directions. The need to revivify the separate convention movement was clear. During these years of full alliance with the whites, however, a new generation of African American leaders had begun to assert itself in local organizations. These men and women, often educated at places like Oberlin or the Oneida Institute, were now directing their energies toward the revived convention. James McCune Smith of New York City, Pennsylvanians John B. Vashon and Martin Delany, James W. C. Pennington and Amos Beman of Hartford, and, later, escapees like Frederick Douglass and Henry Highland Garnet were some of the new participants who furnished the Convention Movement with what it had lacked previously—fresh leadership, managerial skill, and a stable local and regional organization.

From the mid-1840s onward, the Convention Movement attempted to involve average citizens directly in efforts to start schools, develop libraries, promote temperance, and battle discrimination. Later in the 1850s, disputes between Douglass, Delany, and others over the wisdom of black emigration shattered the national organization. Yet the state and local meetings continued through the end of the Civil War, when national leaders reassembled. In the meantime, the Convention Movement provided a forum for leaders to debate ideas, to share in a common race identity, and, most of all, to develop measures to combat oppression. Theirs was a herculean task, and outside of their local communities, their persistence never yielded more than minimal rewards.

Convention leaders spent the most time and resources in an attempt to improve the quality of black education. Programs of self-help were fruitless, argued Martin Delany, if black children did not receive education which fitted them for careers that produced goods and income. Here, indeed, was wise advice in the age of the market revolution. Others, like Samuel Cornish, emphasized high-quality schooling as a socializing device for imparting to African American children the firm moral values of the adult community. Seeking these several ends, blacks throughout the North responded to the convention's call to establish local education groups for young people, like New York's Phoenix Society and the Philomatheon Society of Boston. Offering instruction in various trades, literature, and basic academic skills, these voluntary associations sprang up in Philadelphia, Pittsburgh, Cleveland, Cincinnati, and elsewhere.

White reformers provided financial support for charitable organizations such as these, but decidedly less so as African Americans sought to develop separate colleges and manual-training schools. After an initial flurry of enthusiasm in the

1830s, influential Garrisonians expressed their unremitting hostility to the idea of separate black colleges and worked assiduously to discourage potential contributors. Blacks, too, were split on the question of separation in education, with some leaders like William C. Nell arguing that integrated schools did "mighty work in uprooting prejudice." Others, like Delany, argued that African American children should attend separate colleges and receive training to serve their race's exclusive needs. Internal disagreements were only exacerbated by unsought white opinions like those of Maria Weston Chapman, who denounced all separate academies as "obeisances to slavery."

Similar problems beset the black reformers as they attempted, with marginal success, to establish a national newspaper. Samuel Cornish and John B. Russwurm tried first in 1827 with *Freedom's Journal*, which lasted only two years. Cornish tried again in 1837, over Garrison's loud opposition, with *The Colored American*, which survived on meager readership until 1841. When Douglass finally succeeded in permanently establishing *The North Star* in 1847, it was over loud objections from Boston Garrisonians and thanks to the charity of white philanthropist Gerrit Smith.

Alongside these twin frustrations of white criticism and white charity lay the obvious problem of apathy within the African American community itself. Black newspapers like Cornish's failed because not enough African American readers cared to, or could, support them. Back in 1831, Garrison's *Liberator* had survived largely because Boston's blacks had subscribed to it, but in 1847 Douglass's paper relied on whites for eighty percent of its readership. As early as 1829, David Walker had excoriated his fellow African Americans for their lack of concern, and he would not be the last to do so. How could white society's prejudices ever abate, Walker had asked, "when we are confirming [them] every day by our *groveling submissions* and *treachery?"* But Samuel Ringgold Ward had a point, too, when he placed primary responsibility for black disinterest on the intensity of white racism, which, he was certain, "discourages [a person's] efforts, damps his ardor, blasts his hopes and embitters his spirit." As in their relationships with whites, African American abolitionists were compelled to determine the limits of activism among their own race. It is hardly surprising that they discovered that most Northern blacks were preoccupied with the day-to-day trials of impoverishment, wholly skeptical of the idea of advancing the entire race against the overwhelming forces which blighted the lives of each of them. Granting exceptions like David Walker, it is also little wonder that black abolitionism's leaders exemplified privilege —successful ministers, brilliant fugitive slaves who enjoyed a degree of white patronage, and young, well-educated agitator-intellectuals.

Though uncommitted to militant race solidarity, the African American community did furnish its activist element with a strong and invaluable institution—its churches. Here, more than anywhere else, was where black people turned for physical assistance, psychological support, and discerning leadership. Most white churches ("free churches" set up by white abolitionists in the 1840s were usually an exception) had been segregated long before the eighteenth century. By the 1790s, racist practices among the white Methodists had stimulated the emergence of two separate African American denominations— the Bethel African Methodist Church and the African Methodist Episcopal Church. During the 1820s, black Baptists also formed a separate organization, and as the 1830s opened, every African American population center of consequence supported several active congregations.

Reflecting the inclinations of their members, most churches did not participate openly in black abolitionism. Such was the case even though the African Methodist Episcopal Church barred slaveholders in 1816. Most congregations, however, carried out self-help projects and education programs, as they were urged to by the National Convention Movement. Abolitionist or not, every properly conducted African American church contributed to a sense of community consciousness and race pride. Most black ministers, however, judiciously avoided open association with abolitionism, emphasizing noncontroversial themes of salvation in their sermons, not the sin of slavery.

Yet the ministry furnished black abolitionism with most of its leaders and inspiration. Samuel D. Cornish, Henry Highland Garnet, Theodore S. Wright, and Samuel Ringgold Ward all occupied pulpits in the Methodist or Baptist churches, and this list could be expanded greatly. African American religion in the North, moreover, was pronouncedly evangelical, although its leaders were hardly receptive to the romantic utopianism of the white reformers' religion. Belief in human perfectionism had little relevance to their struggles against exploitation and exclusion. Black evangelicalism most often supported black abolitionism through its emphasis on God's retributive justice, its stress on the brotherhood of all peoples, and its insistence on diligence and personal uprightness.

African American congregations promoted abolition in other ways as well. Churches, for example, served a function about which whites often knew little and in which they participated only secondarily—the protection of fugitive slaves. A white-sponsored "underground railroad" which efficiently spirited fugitives out of slavery existed only in the realm of post-Civil War mythmaking. While prominent whites like Levi Coffin, Samuel J. May, and Gerrit Smith did provide temporary protection for an occasional runaway, it remained largely to African Americans to protect escapees from federal marshals. They did so by using churches and private homes as sites for vigilance societies and as temporary havens for runaways.

New York City's vigilance group, dominated by African Americans and managed until 1840 by tenacious David Ruggles, served as a model for others which arose in many black communities. Before 1850, these groups occasionally greeted slave catchers with physical resistance, as in Detroit in 1833, when a group of outraged blacks assaulted a local sheriff who was detaining accused fugitives. Most, however, initially preferred nonviolent opposition. But after the passage of the 1850 Fugitive Slave Law, which placed every Northern black in jeopardy, premeditated violence became far more commonplace. "The only way to make the fugitive slave law dead letter," Douglass once vowed, "is to make a half a dozen or more dead kidnappers." In the Jerry McHenry rescue, blacks and whites shared some of Douglass's militancy and joined on several other occasions to rescue captives from the federal "bloodhounds."

Yet most who escaped slavery had only themselves and their fellow African Americans to thank. Harriet Tubman, herself a fugitive who operated from Canada, reputedly made more than a dozen forays into the South and brought back more than two hundred people. In Pennsylvania, William Still also engineered slave escapes. Much more commonly, however, runaways relied on their own wits and the help of friendly slaves to escape from the "cotton kingdom," using informal networks of communication first established during the American Revolution. Once in the North, the fugitives would be resettled in relative safety by vigilance groups or assisted through the free states to Canada, where many escapees already lived. Whites knew little, whatever the destination. James G. Birney once remarked that he knew "nothing" of these matters "generally until they are passed."

White abolitionists did not, however, ignore the plight of the fugitives. Charles Turner Torrey, for one, suffered a martyr's fate, dying in a Maryland jail cell after being convicted of abetting the escape of slaves. Captain Daniel Drayton also went to prison for attempting to spirit slaves out of Washington, D.C., in the hold of his merchant ship. But such instances were exceptions, and in Torrey's case it is likely that his actions reflected a pathological desire for martyrdom. White abolitionists usually took a deep interest in fugitives who, like Douglass, were eager to testify to the horrors of slavery. Here were the most authentic witnesses of all, far superior even to former slaveholders like Birney. White audiences turned out in large numbers to hear daring African American speakers describe what their lives had been like under the "peculiar institution."

In this age of romantic sentimentalism, fugitive slaves turned public speakers made perhaps the most effective black contribution to the crusade against slavery. Henry Bibb could move audiences to weeping as he recounted how his wife, naked and bound, had been whipped by her brutal master. The white response to Ellen Craft, a striking light-skinned fugitive, was no less emotional or physically graphic, but was indicative of the dynamics of race and sexuality inherent in white abolitionism. "To think of such a woman being held as a piece of property," exclaimed the white Garrisonian Samuel May, Jr. That so fair-complected and, to whites, so attractive an African American woman was "subject to be traded off to the highest bidder (while in reality no worse than when done to the blackest woman that ever was)" touched even the most prejudiced souls, May believed.

By the 1840s, Douglass, William Wells Brown, Samuel Ringgold Ward, Harriet Tubman, William and Ellen Craft, Sojourner Truth, and many other escaped slaves had taken to lecturing throughout the North. Their narrations of physical abuse and privation, of separation from loved ones, and of emotional distress forced whites to remember the conditions faced daily by over two million people still enslaved. Yet, as May's comments regarding Ellen Craft indicate, black fugitive-activists faced the problem of being viewed by whites as useful theatrical exhibits. When Douglass was refining his rhetorical skills, members of the American Anti-Slavery Society feared for his authenticity, since he now appeared too "learned." "People won't believe you were ever a slave, Frederick," Garrison warned. Parker Pillsbury added that it was "better [to] have a *little* of the plantation manner of speech than not."

Such white directiveness quite often accompanied the assistance so necessary in launching careers like Douglass's. And there was no question of the need for aid. Wealthy, literate, commanding the lecture circuits, and enjoying full access to the printing press, the white reformers had the capacity to help the careers of fugitive-activists. White abolitionists commonly collaborated with fugitives, editing or ghostwriting their slave narratives and subsidizing publication. William Wells Brown, for example, asked Edmund Quincy, a white Garrisonian, to edit his manuscript. White abolitionists in turn were anxious that the narratives be factually correct; by the mid-1840s, slave memoirs had achieved a tremendous readership. Douglass's *Autobiography* (written without assistance) sold widely in the 1850s.

The slaves' narratives gave Northern whites a comprehensive picture of life in slavery, countering easy stereotype with brutal reality. Along with depictions of mistreatment were portraits of stable slave families presided over by resourceful men and women who acquired skills, created institutions, and satisfied material needs on their own. In recent decades, historians have confirmed the accuracy of these narratives, using them and other data to reconstruct African American culture in slavery. By stressing the slaves' humanity, their cultural vitality, and their accomplishments, slave narratives contested prevailing racial myths far more comprehensively than any other kind of abolitionist literature.

Considering the extent of racism in the dominant culture, it is hardly surprising that feelings of alienation against all white society surfaced early among a few African American abolitionists. The men who revived the National Convention Movement in 1843 had sensed the inadequacy of white reform. A much more ominous symptom of estrangement was the increasing willingness of powerful spokesmen like Henry Highland Garnet and Samuel Ringgold Ward to invoke the memory of Nat Turner. Indeed, at the 1843 convention Garnet delivered "An Address to the Slaves of the United States of America" which urged rebellion against the masters and quoted from David Walker's *Appeal.* Frederick Douglass and Charles Remond opposed Garnet's call, but largely on grounds of expediency — revolt in the South would risk a bloodbath there and further jeopardize free blacks everywhere. By 1849, Douglass had changed his position, announcing that he would welcome insurrection. The next year, African American leaders moved further toward violence, responding to the Fugitive Slave Law by vowing to resist the slave catchers with force. Vigilance societies multiplied, circulating Walker's *Appeal* to their members. Intrepid men like Garnet carried side arms. In black circles during the 1850s, endorsements of defensive and revolutionary violence transformed alienation into something far different.

This siege mentality expressed itself most forcefully in espousals of nationalism and proposals for emigration. The origins of antebellum black nationalism can be traced to the 1830s, to the ideas of Lewis Woodson, an early preceptor of Martin Delany. Emigrationist projects developed by African Americans also date to an earlier time, 1815, when shipowner Paul Cuffee sent thirty-eight free blacks to Sierra Leone. But until the 1850s most black leaders equated emigration with the hated American Colonization Society. Nationalism had also been a minor theme in African American ideology. Once the new Fugitive Slave Law took force, however, some nine thousand Northern blacks fled to Canada. Soon after, emigrationists began holding national conventions. Besides debating the merits of moving to Haiti, the Gold Coast, or Mexican California, they emphasized their conviction that reform within the United States was impossible. Now, they stressed, the destiny of the black race lay in building a new and just civilization, which would war against the African slave trade and all forms of inherited servitude.

By the late 1850s, many African American spokesmen, especially Garnet, Ward, and Alexander Crummell, were involved in emigrationism. Even Douglass, who normally stood foursquare for continuing the struggle on American soil, investigated the possibility of founding an emigrant colony in Haiti. It was Martin Delany, however, who emerged as emigrationism's most serious proponent. A Harvard-educated physician, Delany supported emigrationism, identifying with black revolutionaries of the past, especially Nat Turner, Denmark Vesey, and Toussaint L'Ouverture. In his incomplete novel, *Blake*, the central character is a black guerrilla warrior kidnapped from Cuba into the Deep South. There Blake foments revolt, encouraged by associates with memories of Nat Turner's stirring days, for whom racial unity is the vital ingredient of successful revolution. Delany himself, convinced that the destiny of blacks lay in Africa, led an expedition up the Niger River in 1859 to map likely sites for settlement.

Nothing came of Delany's efforts, however, and after 1861 espousals of emigration and nationalism temporarily ceased. War and emancipation rekindled in African American abolitionists a hope that white America was capable of transformation. The significance of the militancy of the 1850s lies not in projects completed or revolutions begun. In Delany's specific plans, as in the general endorsements of black exodus, alienation had crystallized into a sweeping ideology that transcended national identity. Considering the frustrations that drove African Americans from white abolitionism, it is note-worthy that the two groups joined forces as often as they did and with such substantial results.

Black and white reformers discovered early that collabora-tion was easiest and most effective in campaigns to combat legal and customary discrimination. In challenges to segregated public schools, jim-crow public accommodations, and legisla-tive disenfranchisement, the whites' insistence on moral abso-lutes and the African Americans' practical goal of mitigating oppression harmonized nicely. Whites like William Lloyd Gar-rison who burned to bear witness to "truth" could work along-side blacks like Frederick Douglass whose vital interest was easing caste oppression as best they could. An incident during the summer of 1841 in New Bedford, Massachusetts, shows how the process worked.

In June, David Ruggles, the militant director of the New York City Vigilance Committee, refused to sit in the blacks-only section of a steamer bound for Nantucket. The next month, Ruggles was back, this time boarding the "white car" of the New Bedford railway. After being dragged from the car, Ruggles took the railway to court, and local blacks threatened anti-discrimination suits. The judge held in favor of the rail-road, whereupon Garrison and his white friends rushed to New Bedford to denounce the decision. On August 9, Garrison and Douglass, along with forty other black and white aboli-tionists, boarded a steamer from which Ruggles had also been ejected. On this particular day the captain relented, and the integrated group climbed up to the open-air Negro deck to enjoy the sunshine and hold an antislavery meeting, complete with speeches and resolutions condemning segregation. It was a pleasant outing, and the two abolitionisms had indeed rein-forced each other well. Soon individual acts of civil disobedi-ence as well as concerted efforts by integrated groups became common throughout New England.

These protests were not always so cheerfully nonviolent. African Americans who entered the whites-only sections of public conveyances invited treatment that whites who defied segregation usually escaped. In Lynn, Massachusetts, Mary Green, holding a baby, was dragged out of a whites-only railroad car, struck, and hurled to the ground. Her husband, daring to intervene, was beaten. White abolitionists experienced this sort of handling only when accompanied by black associates. When Wendell Phillips invaded segregated train cars alone, with African American companions, or with other whites, the conductors sullenly pretended not to notice.

In our time, when theoretical equality under the law remains controverted by the brutal reality of discrimination, it is tempting to dismiss a long-ago victory over segregated transportation in Massachusetts as devoid of enduring significance. Yet to play a role in the abolition of cramped, rancid "nigger" railway cars was to liberate oneself from humiliating experiences and group debasement. Most abolitionists, whatever their race, understood their boycotts, lawsuits, and acts of civil disobedience as integral to moral suasion — public appeals which transcended local issues and confronted the white North with its racism. One can only speculate what American race relations might have been like if such efforts had not been made.

At the time, abolitionists struggled against degrading separatism because desegregation held out the important promise of better education for young people in the North. In some states like Ohio and Illinois, which legislated against African Americans in public education, activists of both races raised funds to establish private schools. In some cases, black children and white did try to join in the same public-school classrooms, but physical abuse and educational disaster were the only visible results. Many black parents then requested segregated facilities and agitated for their improvement. But, most often, black and white abolitionists joined forces in boycotts, lawsuits, and civil disobedience, with school desegregation as their immediate goal.

During the 1840s, many local African Americans successfully boycotted segregated schools, with considerable assistance from whites. White Garrisonians participated openly in a boycott in Nantucket, Massachusetts, while in Salem the former mayor, Stephen C. Phillips, an influential Conscience Whig, also sided with the boycotters there. In Rochester, Douglass enlisted his white colleagues in protracted battles which technically ended separate and unequal public schools in that city.

The most significant struggles for desegregation in public education centered in Boston and brought together some of the antislavery crusade's already famous whites and previously obscure African Americans. The conflict in Boston took root in 1829 when the mayor purposely neglected to invite a fully deserving black honors student, William C. Nell, to a city-sponsored banquet recognizing outstanding seniors. By the mid-1840s, Nell, who was then working as the office manager for Garrison's *Liberator*, repaid this slight by leading a protracted campaign to integrate Boston's schools. Inspired by the success of the Salem boycott in 1844, Nell enlisted another African American abolitionist whose children attended segregated schools, John T. Hilton, and together they began a petition campaign directed at the Boston school committee. When petitions failed, boycotts began, stimulated by the fact that one of the white teachers in an all-black school administered excessive punishments and was habitually absent from class.

Horace Mann, secretary of the Massachusetts Board of Education, tried without success to work out a compromise, while school authorities continued to reject the petitions of Nell's Friends of Equal School Rights Society. When Mann tried to ease the situation by appointing a new black principal in one of the segregated schools, Nell and Hilton called forth the parents, surrounded the school, and attempted to prevent students from registering. Police drove them away from the schoolyard and the African American principal took office, but the boycott of segregated schools remained in force until April 1855, when the state government finally outlawed all distinctions of color and religion in Massachusetts schools. Eleven years of African American persistence had resulted in the first statewide desegregation decision in American history. Black leaders were predominant throughout, and white abolitionists proved their worth as loyal supporters, not patronizing critics.

The boycotts also involved the desegregation effort in two expensive court suits. Here, white expertise proved most valuable. In 1849, African American attorney Robert Morris and Massachusetts' leading Free-Soiler, Charles Sumner, brought a lawsuit, known as the Roberts Case, against the Boston school committee's segregationist policies. Appealing adverse lower-court rulings before the State Supreme Court in 1850, Sumner and Morris argued without success most of the grounds which were to be adopted by the plaintiffs one hundred and four years later in the 1954 *Brown v. Board of Education of Topeka* desegregation suit, in which the United States Supreme Court finally found segregation to be unconstitutional. On many similar occasions, other white attorneys such as Salmon P. Chase put their services at the disposal of blacks ensnared by the North's highly prejudiced legal system. Just as in the sit-ins and boycotts, the two abolitionisms interacted without friction to benefit the cause. Sectional figures of high standing found opportunity to express genuine humanitarian concern while trumpeting their opposition to the "slave power's" mastery of American law. Black defendants, fortunate to be expertly represented, at least had a better chance to have a fair hearing. Yet none of these victories, valuable as they were, did anything to hasten the day of emancipation in the South.

With this fact much on his mind, Frederick Douglass attended the Buffalo convention of the Free-Soil Party in the summer of 1848. Surrounded by racist Van Burenites like David Wilmot (author of the famous free-soil proviso), dedicated reformers like Joshua Leavitt, and sincere but partial friends of black freedom like Joshua Giddings, he must have experienced strong feelings of ambivalence. The New York Liberty men in attendance, original immediatists like Leavitt, Henry B. Stanton, and Alvan Stewart, had campaigned hard in that state's referendum two years earlier to remove restrictions on the right of African American men to vote — just one of many instances when white Liberty men supported efforts to repeal laws against blacks. But white supremacy was rapidly emerging as a central theme in the ideology of political antislavery. The presence of Martin Van Buren, once the abolitionists' most bitter political enemy, testified to that. So did well-timed warnings from Garrisonians that racist overtones permeated the politicians' cries for "free soil." Nevertheless, Douglass could see with absolute clarity that the power to free the slaves lay in the rough-and-tumble of racist free-soil politics, not in the meetings of Boston's Garrisonians or among the congregations of the city's militant black churches. After reflecting on these facts and assessing the risks, Douglass endorsed Martin Van Buren for President in the 1848 elections, observing quite aptly that "what is morally right is not always politically possible." Over the next decade, from the perspective of African American activists, the distance between the morally right and the politically possible would only grow steadily greater.

7

ABOLITIONISTS AND THE
COMING OF THE CIVIL WAR

Early in 1857, William Lloyd Garrison and John Brown met for the only time in Theodore Parker's home. Though Parker and Garrison were unaware of the fact, it had been at Brown's hands six months earlier that five unarmed settlers in Kansas had been brutally murdered in the dead of night — shot, their corpses then hacked at with swords, their bodies left along Pottawatomie Creek. Since 1854, the struggle between free-staters and Southerners over the possible expansion of slavery in Kansas had claimed the lives of several Free-Soilers who had settled there. In murdering five immigrants from the slave states, Brown had envisioned himself as God's bloody avenger. Little wonder that Brown and Garrison could find no agreement as they debated one of Garrison's favorite topics — Christian non-resistance. Each time Garrison referred to the pacifism of Jesus, Brown, inwardly sneering at such "milk and water" abolitionism, countered with the bloody prophecies of Jeremiah.

In the years immediately following the Compromise of 1850, until 1854 at least, the violent atmosphere created by Brown and his Kansas opponents would have been hard to predict. The compromise, accepted grudgingly at first by many politicians, quickly became an acomplishment they wished preserved at all cost. Shaken by their recent flirtations with sectional disaster, unionist politicians everywhere vowed that the compromise legislation constituted a "permanent solution" to slavery questions.

Events seemed to bear out this view. In every Northern state during the early 1850s, the Free-Soil Party began to fall apart, merging its organizations with one of the two major parties in exchange for offices and programs. An independent Free-Soil Party did compete in the 1852 Presidential contest, but its vote was small and its impact on the election was minimal as Democrat Franklin Pierce overwhelmed the Whigs' Winfield Scott. By 1853, an organized antislavery third party was all but absent from politics.

Equally cheering to both slaveholders and pro-slavery Northerners was the renewed interest of many Yankees in holding unionist meetings and mobbing abolitionists. In New York City, businessmen and merchants organized a Union Safety Committee to disrupt the May 1850 meeting of the American Anti-Slavery Society and to express solidarity with their business associates in the slave states. In Tammany Hall ward boss Isaiah Rynders, these "gentlemen of property and standing" found a person able and eager to mobilize the anti-abolitionist lower-class Irish of New York. When the abolitionists attempted to convene at the Broadway Tabernacle, harassment began and Rynders's bullies stormed the rostrum. True to their principles of non-resistance, the Garrisonians did nothing to defend themselves.

It seemed to "friends of the Union" a return to the more reassuring days of the early 1830s: abolitionists reduced to a noisy handful, no disruptive anti-Southern third party in national elections, Whigs and Democrats competing for office on sectionally non-controversial economic issues. Yet it is hard to imagine a more misleading conclusion. Despite appearances, anti-Southern feeling continued to spread in the Northern wings of both parties during the early 1850s. Abolitionists, meanwhile, grew increasingly eager to confront the problem of slavery with threats of violence.

As Free-Soil leaders jockeyed with Whigs and Democrats in the state legislatures during the early 1850s, non-voting Garrisonians kept up their now-traditional criticism, condemning third-party adherents for their willingness to compromise. Political abolitionists like Gamaliel Bailey, now editor of the influential Washington-based *National Era*, once again gave general support to these coalition maneuvers, but pressed the Free-Soilers not to lose sight of higher antislavery goals.

Whether the abolitionists approved or not, it was clear that the Free-Soilers' negotiations with the major parties made significant gains for political antislavery. Sectional politics were developing a momentum of their own, apart from abolitionist activity. The process made the Whigs and Democrats even more vulnerable to sectional disruption than they had been prior to the 1850 Compromise. Quietly now, in the absence of dramatic conflict in Washington, divisive sectional forces ate away at the traditional two-party system.

In Massachusetts, an impressive collaboration between Free-Soilers and Democrats sent to the United States Senate elegant Charles Sumner, widely noted for his bombastic speeches against slaveholding, his close ties to Garrisonians, and his courtroom attacks on segregation. "By the license of slavery," he once declared on the Senate floor, "a whole race is delivered over to prostitution and concubinage, without the protection of any law." A close associate of militants like Wendell Phillips and Theodore Parker, Sumner read Garrison's *Liberator* devotedly and maintained close ties with antislavery politicians like Joshua Giddings and Salmon P. Chase. Indeed, one can see in Sumner's 1851 election to the Senate a telling sign of anti-slavery coalition and a portent of the wrenching sectional

divisions to come. In Ohio, meanwhile, a Whig–Free-Soil coalition set up in 1851 allowed another great pocket of antislavery constituents to elect a senator. In that year, the two parties
combined to launch Benjamin Wade's career as a blunt-spoken
foe of the "slave power." In 1849, through a similar process of
"horse-trading," Free-Soil cooperation with the Democrats had
elected Chase, former Liberty Party leader, as senator.
Throughout the 1850s, no state save Massachusetts matched
Ohio's senatorial delegation in its antagonism toward the
South. Calling themselves Independent Democrats, Free Democrats, or Free-Soil Whigs, these new senators and representatives provided an accurate measure of Northern politics'
continued sectionalization after the crisis of 1850. Such political labels further indicated that many Northern voters as well
as their party leaders now made opposition to the "slave
power" a prerequisite of their continuing allegiance to the two-
party system.

Although to the supporters of the 1850 Compromise calm
seemed to prevail in politics, the structures supporting the
American party system were being undermined by sectionalism. In the South no less than in the North, neither party
seemed able to rally its supporters around economic issues such
as banking and tariff policy which had once reinforced intersectional allegiances. In the absence of such stabilizing factors,
one more serious disagreement over slavery might just destroy
sectional equilibrium and invite upheaval. Sensing this, and
driven by frustration, many abolitionists discarded their pacifism and sought forceful confrontations with the pro-slavery
government.

More than two decades earlier, abolitionists had held very
different opinions about violence. The original immediatists of
the 1830s had organized as forthrightly nonviolent, promoting
moral suasion, not the application of force, in their efforts to
free the slaves. At the time, their choice had been both wise

and ethical. Peaceful tactics had harmonized with the broader creeds of evangelical religion and Quakerism from which the abolitionists had drawn their inspiration. In an age that exalted the forceful leader, favored the slaveowner, and condoned the mob, the abolitionists' radicalness was based in their peaceful appeals to conscience.

Immediatists had also adopted pacifism for compelling practical reasons. Founded in an atmosphere rife with the fear of slave revolts, the American Anti-Slavery Society had been well advised to make clear its abhorrence of black insurrection. As a despised minority surrounded by powerful pro-slavery interests, abolitionists had been counseled by prudence as well as principle to respond as pacifists to mob assault. Until the 1850s, any widespread attempt by abolitionists to promote violence would have called down a wave of repression even more brutal than what they had actually endured. But abolitionists who endorsed nonviolence for practical reasons would obviously feel free to discard the tactic whenever desperate circumstances seemed to justify doing so. For some abolitionists, the pro-slavery triumphs of the early 1850s were such a compelling reason.

Apart from these tactical considerations, abolitionists held to basic tenets that could be reformulated to justify violence. One such tenet, John Brown's favorite, involved the biblical theme of God's raining bloody vengeance on His hard-hearted people. Another path to violence led through the doctrines of the Liberty Party, which Garrisonian non-resistants perceptively criticized as manipulations of political power that could easily justify the use of naked force. Even long-confirmed pacifists like William Lloyd Garrison and Steven S. Foster found that they could twist their principles to justify bloody deeds. Foster, for example, felt he was speaking as a sincere non-resistant when he stated that "every man should act on his own convictions, whether he believed in using moral or physical force."

Hence, Foster argued, he himself was free to urge others to kill the kidnappers of fugitive slaves, and to call the slaves to arms.

Abolitionists also realized quite vividly just how little their long crusade had actually accomplished, an assessment that seemed to make the use of violence all the more attractive. Two decades of preaching against the sin of slavery had yielded, not emancipation, but an increase to over four hundred thousand black people held in bondage. Despite arduous espousals of "moral revolution," the area of the slave states had expanded enormously, automatically guaranteeing the growth of the "slave power" in all aspects of American life. At the same time, America's moral sensitivity certainly seemed to abolitionists to have narrowed.

Liberty men such as James G. Birney and Gerrit Smith recalled their earnest efforts early in the 1840s to make the electoral process serve humanity, and they shuddered at the results. Abolitionism, as an independent force in politics, seemed to have taken a downward course, from the hopeful days of the one-idea emancipationist platform, through the Free-Soil compromise with the racist Van Burenites, to near extinction. Birney's disillusion drove him into bitter seclusion in the Michigan forest, from which he counseled African Americans to flee the United States. Smith found solace in the minuscule Liberty League, in helping to finance John Brown's bloody work in Kansas, and in defying the Fugitive Slave Law. African American militants like Henry Highland Garnet preached insurrection or, like Martin Delany, abandoned all hope for the future of black people on American soil. Ann Greene Phillips, an astute Boston abolitionist, perhaps best summed up the frustration, desperation, and rage which were fast overtaking many abolitionists when she commented: "We may as well disband at once, if our meetings and papers are all talk and we never do anything but talk."

Symbolizing the nation's continuing embrace of evil, the new Fugitive Slave Law drew the unremitting hostility of militant abolitionists throughout the 1850s. From the moment of its enactment, abolitionists of both races and serious antislavery politicians throughout the North announced their determination to oppose it — with raw force, if necessary. "We cannot be Christians and obey it," Congressman Joshua R. Giddings warned bluntly. Veteran African American abolitionists like Samuel Ringgold Ward agreed with Giddings; many of them had long ago concluded that "the right and duty of the oppressed to destroy their oppressors," as Ward put it, was sanctioned by "God's Holy Writ." When white abolitionist Samuel J. May also decided to endorse violence, this measured acutely just how completely militants had captured the abolitionist movement. Until the 1850s, May had maintained an impressive record of Christian pacifism in the face of every kind of provocation. Yet he, like Giddings and Ward, told his parishioners in 1851 that they were under holy "obligation" to defy the law by force of arms if necessary, just "as you are not to lie, steal and murder."

By advocating the use of violence against the Fugitive Slave Law, abolitionists found themselves ever more deeply involved in the broader Northern struggle in politics against the "slave power." The many disagreements that had for so long separated Garrisonian abolitionists from Free-Soilers, Whigs and Democrats from Liberty Leaguers, and black abolitionists from whites vanished as antislavery Northerners of every persuasion established an unprecedented collaborative resistance to slave catchers. Since their acts of defiance against the state did not touch off a wave of repression or stimulate conservative turns in the public's attitude, as they had in the 1830s, each incident only quickened the tempo of resistance. The more strident the abolitionists made their opposition to the Fugitive Slave Law, the more widespread was Northern resentment of the "slave power." Especially for slaveholders, distinctions between abolitionists, politicians, and ordinary Northern citizens were becoming increasingly difficult to maintain.

To be sure, abolitionists of both races had tried to make good on pledges to aid fugitives long before the passage of the 1850 law. Whites had helped, while blacks organized vigilance societies, harassed sheriffs, and relocated escapees. Anger at Northern involvement in slave-hunting was hardly new either, as attested by the personal-liberty laws passed in various free states during the 1830s and 1840s. What was changed after 1850 was the intensity and pervasiveness of Northern resistance. A new generation of Beechers — Charles and Henry Ward, sons of the towering evangelical leader Lyman Beecher — led a host of eloquent young ministers who preached of "higher laws" than those of Congress to which the practicing Christian owed first allegiance. Immediatist ministers like Samuel J. May, Theodore Parker, and Thomas Wentworth Higginson furnished examples of "practical Christianity" by engaging publicly in acts of defiance that were filled with violent overtones.

May had taken a hand directly when a mob forcibly rescued fugitive Jerry McHenry from the Syracuse jail. Still claiming to uphold nonviolence, May nevertheless confided to Garrison feelings which many other non-resistants were coming to share: "When I saw poor Jerry in the hands of the official kidnappers, I could not preach nonresistance very earnestly to the crowd who were clamoring for his release." In 1850, Theodore Parker, who never claimed to be a pacifist, took command of the Boston Vigilance Committee, which now included Thomas Wentworth Higginson, Wendell Phillips, Samuel Gridley Howe, and the black escapee Lewis Hayden. In 1851, the muscular Hayden led a group of militant African Americans into a Boston courtroom and forcibly rescued a much-surprised fugitive, Fred Wilkins (known locally as Shadrach). Parker, ecstatic, praised the deed as the "noblest done in Boston since the destruction of the tea." Higginson, who was running for Congress at the time as a Free-Soil Democrat, likewise publicly defended Hayden's bold display of force. In September 1851, when a group of African Americans in Christiana, Pennsylvania, fatally shot a federal marshal who attempted to seize one of their number, Parker, Phillips, Douglass, and Higginson all called with enthusiasm for more such scenes. Hayden, for his part, began wearing a pistol.

The fugitive-slave incident which probably illustrates most clearly the unification of militant antislavery forces involved the unfortunate Thomas Sims. After a fierce struggle, federal marshals in Boston seized Sims, an escapee from Georgia, in April 1851. The Boston Vigilance Committee convened hurriedly, and non-resistants like Garrison contributed pacifist suggestions as Phillips, Parker, Higginson, and Hayden considered various strategies to free the captive. As a hundred and fifty policemen surrounded the courthouse in which Sims was held, antislavery politicians came forward to seek Sims's release through legal appeals. Among them were Samuel Sewall, founding member of the American Anti-Slavery Society and later a Liberty man, and soon to be United States Senator-elect Charles Sumner.

Legal proceedings ensued, and the Vigilance Committee organized protest meetings, which antislavery partisans of nearly every description eagerly attended. Horace Mann, now a Free-Soil Whig congressman, presided over the meeting in Tremont Temple, and Samuel Gridley Howe, a Vigilance Committee member with violence on his mind, convened the meeting. The speakers included the old immediatist Elizur Wright, Jr., the aspiring Free-Soil politician and soon to be United States Senator Henry Wilson, and two apostles of force — the disunionist Wendell Phillips and the radical Unitarian minister Thomas Wentworth Higginson. Theirs was a most notable assembly of militants. Some among them counseled law and order, but Higginson, with "fire in the eye," made his listeners tremble with his calls for violent resistance. "We were on the eve of revolution with that speech," Phillips recalled.

That the gathering ultimately endorsed a due regard for law and order in no way diminishes a far more important fact: antislavery politicians and abolitionists were openly opposing federal authority, debating the limits of peaceful dissent, and exploring the imperatives of forcible resistance. In the process, immediatist radicals were becoming increasingly difficult to distinguish from sectionally aroused politicians; their function as reformers became ever more linked to their ability to add to the atmosphere of sectional crisis. For example, when all his legal appeals failed, the lawyer-politician Charles Sumner agreed with the Vigilance Committee's last, desperate (and unworkable) plan to intercept and forcibly board the slave ship which was to transport Sims back to Georgia.

Despite the commotion generated by acts of resistance, the Fugitive Slave Law was never rendered unenforceable, as scholars once claimed. In parts of New England, in upstate New York, and in the Western Reserve, citizens did flout the law openly and received fugitives with great ceremony. In April 1859, for example, when some daring federal marshals ventured into Oberlin and seized a fugitive slave, a mob of students, faculty, and irate townsfolk rescued the captive and were later acquitted by a local jury. Yet, on many occasions, escapees were quickly arrested before local antislavery forces had a chance to prevent it. Especially in southern Ohio, Indiana, Illinois, and Pennsylvania, abolitionist leadership was nonexistent, and citizens complied willingly with the marshals. As the abortive efforts to rescue Thomas Sims demonstrated, furthermore, policemen and magistrates could provide the marshals with considerable support. Most formidable to the "foes of the slave power" was the obvious determination of President

Franklin Pierce to enforce the law with massive federal power.

Logically, Pierce chose defiant Boston as the site for his display of federal authority. On May 25, 1854, a well-educated young fugitive named Anthony Burns was arrested, the first in Boston since Thomas Sims. Again the Vigilance Committee convened, the protest meetings gathered, and Phillips and Parker all but urged violent action to end Burns's captivity. Suddenly, a cry rang out that hundreds of men, led by Higginson, were storming the courthouse; they threw bricks, battered down the front door, and rushed inside to seek out Anthony Burns. Instead, they were confronted by the courthouse guards, and at the height of the melee one guard was fatally shot. The police arrived and began arresting rioters. The mayor requested federal troops and the chief of police received a telegram from Pierce: "Your conduct is approved. The law must be executed." Several days later Higginson, now himself a fugitive from an arrest warrant, mounted the pulpit to announce: "I can only make my life worth living for, by becoming a revolutionist."

Yet Higginson was no more able to aid Burns than were the Garrisonian non-resistants who had expressed dismay at his violent comportment. All the armed forces which the President of the United States could muster in Boston lined the route from the courthouse to the wharf as Burns, surrounded by marshals, was led to the ship which returned him to the South. The soldiers sang the popular tune "Carry Me Back to Old Virginia" while escorting Burns through the streets.

Stark in its drama and frightening in its implications, the sight of armed federal troops occupying the streets of Boston against its own "freedom-loving" citizens greatly intensified long-accumulating fears of the "slave power's" intentions. Pierce's actions (like Jackson's anti-abolitionism in the 1830s) suggested strongly that the office of the President itself, the army he commanded, the powers of executive order and veto he enjoyed, and the party system that supported him, had all been placed at the exclusive disposal of the planter class. Northerners in both major parties wondered increasingly whether any civil liberties remained under firm guarantee, or whether republican freedom existed at all apart from the generosity of the slaveholders. Militants like Parker challenged their audiences: "We are the vassals of Virginia. It reaches its arm over the graves of our mothers, it kidnaps men in the city of Puritans, over the graves of Samuel Adams and John Hancock."

Moved by these feelings, Garrison endowed his oft-declared disunionism with a new, more bellicose tone. On July 4, 1854, in Framingham, Massachusetts, he ceremoniously burned, first a copy of the Fugitive Slave Law, then a copy of the court decision which ordered Anthony Burns's reenslavement, and, finally, a copy of the United States Constitution. The abolitionists who looked on cheered wildly. Moderate antislavery men and women often deplored Garrison's "excesses," but all sectionally sensitive Northerners understood clearly the symbolism of this ritual. The gap which, most antislavery voters claimed, separated them from abolitionist extremism narrowed accordingly.

The militancy of Parker's remarks and Garrison's rituals was linked to the most venerable of American patriotic traditions, historical values which had always inspired the abolitionists' crusade. In the minds of slavery's most bitter opponents, the ties between their day-to-day struggles and America's Revolution grew ever more compelling. When they flouted the law, burned the Constitution, and courted violence, leaders like Parker, Phillips, Garrison, and Higginson felt themselves to be extensions of the original Sons of Liberty and they envisioned themselves reasserting the very principles of freedom for which their grandfathers had fought.

Throughout the 1850s, Phillips constantly invoked the memory of Crispus Attucks and Sam Adams as he urged his listeners to greet the federal marshals as the Patriots had welcomed the Redcoats on Lexington Green. With a similar end in view, African American abolitionist and Boston Vigilance Committee member William Nell published his extraordinary *Colored Patriots of the American Revolution*, a detailed, passionate account of African American heroism in the face of British "tyranny" and a founding document in African American history. Likewise using the Revolution as precedent, Joshua Giddings organized in his home county a Vigilance Committee, the Sons of Liberty, which was dedicated to meeting slave catchers with lethal force.

These developments confirmed the slaveholders' most frightening suspicions, especially after political mavericks like Giddings, Henry Wilson, Horace Mann, and Charles Sumner joined with unabashed radicals like Phillips and Parker in their protests. Despite their disavowals of "abolitionist extremism," what really distinguished Free-Soil politicians from the most extravagant Garrisonians? Free-Soilers claimed to oppose only the westward progress of slavery; but how did their militant appeals to "higher law" and their invitation to "irrepressible conflict" differ from the intentions of a Wendell Phillips? Besides, was it not apparent to Sumner and the rest that halting the expansion of slavery would force the South into moral capitulation, inviting social upheaval?

Viewed from the plantation, Benjamin Wade, Charles Sumner, and Henry Wilson appeared no less threatening than leaders of the American Anti-Slavery Society like Garrison. Yet Northern Whigs and Democrats seemed eager to deal with these "abolitionists in disguise," as one slaveholder called them, and even created senatorships for Wade, Sumner, and Salmon P. Chase, all men who collaborated openly with abolitionists. Was not such behavior evidence that the Northern branches of the two parties were *both* falling victim to abolitionist madness? In the early 1850s, planters pressed for stronger safe-guards, once again demanding access to Western lands, which would guarantee the political predominance of slavery within the Union.

Second only to the menacing John Brown and his sons, the family most responsible for heightening Southerners' anxieties was undoubtedly the Beechers. Ever since the mid-1830s, all but Catherine Beecher had made their family name synony-mous with clerical abolitionism. Lyman Beecher had provoked family dissent in 1835 when he attempted to oppose the Lane Seminary rebels. Two years later in Alton, Illinois, Lyman's oldest son, Edward Beecher, had mounted a vocal defense of abolitionism as the ill-fated Elijah P. Lovejoy prepared to do battle with the mob. In 1850, two other sons, Henry Ward Beecher and Charles Beecher, preached non-compliance with the Fugitive Slave Law. Yet it was quiet Harriet Beecher, now married to Calvin Stowe, who proved the most unsettling of all to the planter class. In 1852, Gamaliel Bailey's *National Era* began weekly installments of her novel *Uncle Tom's Cabin*. While abolitionists, politicians, and black runaways joined in resistance to the Fugitive Slave Law, literate people all over the North read avidly of the tribulations endured by Uncle Tom, George and Eliza Harris, and the others during their years as slaves.

A central event in the history of popular literature, *Uncle Tom's Cabin* made hostility to slavery routine in family enter-tainment. Throughout the North, clever entrepreneurs set about inventing dances, composing songs, and orchestrating dramatic readings based on the book. In the 1830s, abolition-ism had appropriated the techniques of mass journalism; after 1852, hostility to the "slave power" permeated the carnival world of popular melodrama and the traveling stage show.

The plot and characterizations of *Uncle Tom's Cabin* seemed to satisfy every antislavery taste. For non-resistants and for those given to sentimental racism, there was ever-forgiving, ever-Christian Uncle Tom, meeting force with pious submission; for those attracted by militancy and by images of violent black masculinity, there was gun-wielding George Harris, the desperate fugitive; for activist women, Eliza Harris combined beauty, bravery, and independence with a fierce devotion to family and home; for racist Free-Soilers, there were Stowe's expressions of support for colonization and her rich racial stereotypes; for proponents of free labor who abhorred the planter class, there were Tom's first owners, Shelby and St. Clare, well meaning but effeminate, dissipated, and improvident, enervated by lives of slothful dependence on their bondsmen; and for Northerners who felt complicitous for whatever reason in maintaining the "peculiar institution," there was Simon Legree, the Yankee slave-trader, unsurpassed in his wanton brutality.

Stowe's sole contact with slavery had been a few hours spent on a Kentucky plantation. Slave narratives and Theodore D. Weld's *American Slavery As It Is* had provided her only background information. Stowe did command, however, an exact sense of Northern Protestant culture — its evangelical piety, its domesticity, its deeper gender tensions, its sentimentalism, its race prejudice, and, above all, its suspicion of the ways of the plantation. The book could not be printed fast enough to satisfy Northern demands. In the first year after publication, over three hundred thousand copies were sold in the United States alone. In England, *Uncle Tom's Cabin* sold over a million copies before 1861. White Southerners set about feverishly to reply to Stowe's work with hapless literary productions such as *Aunt Phyllis's Cabin*.

But there was little that Southern whites could do to stop people in the North from reading what they chose. They also could not prevent the election of antislavery senators, suppress the incidents of defiance against the Fugitive Slave Law, deny

Wendell Phillips's success as the North's most popular public speaker, or block the British efforts to stamp out slavery in Latin America. Slaveholders had but one recourse as they sought to guarantee the safety of their regime — to wrest further concessions from the North.

Desperately aware that they were in a minority, that Free-Soil abolitionism was making serious inroads in both parties, and that their base of political power was shrinking, influential planters pressured Franklin Pierce and the Democratic Party leadership to open new Western lands to slavery. Accordingly, in January 1854, Stephen A. Douglas sponsored a bill in Congress that would apply the doctrine of popular sovereignty in Kansas and Nebraska, leading to the possible expansion of slave territories previously declared free as part of the 1820 Missouri Compromise. In so doing, he upset forever the tenuous political equilibrium established by the 1850 Compromise, undermined the already weakened two-party system, and set the nation ever more firmly on a course toward civil war.

What prompted Douglas to embrace so disruptive a course? Historians cite his burning Presidential ambitions, which could never be satisfied without Southern support, his interest in Western railroad projects which required the rapid admission of the Kansas–Nebraska territory, and his insensitivity to the tensions which surrounded slavery issues. He later remarked that he cared little whether slavery was "voted up or down" in the territories. Yet Douglas surely knew that his Kansas–Nebraska Bill would, as he himself put it, "raise a hell of a storm." To him the storm seemed eminently worth braving if, through popular sovereignty, sectional disputes could be settled locally, not in Congress. National politics could then be forced back to its traditional principles of sectional bipartisanship and to silence on slave questions. And he was certain that popular sovereignty would result in the peaceful creation of more new free states than slave states.

These were vain hopes. Douglas's bill destroyed the Whig Party and grievously damaged the Northern Democrats. As Southern Whigs joined the Democrats in backing the Kansas–Nebraska Bill, Chase, Sumner, Giddings, Wade, and Gerrit Smith (who, through an unusual Liberty League–Free Soil coalition, had been elected to Congress) issued a forceful appeal to the voters of the North, warning of a "monstrous plot" to turn free territory into "a dreary region of despotism, inhabited by masters and slaves." Frontier lands once reserved by law for free white labor were now to be given as tribute to the insatiable "slave power," they warned. Editors and orators throughout the North embellished these themes, and the nation's political structure fragmented. Sectionalism had finally sapped the resilience of the two-party system. By late 1854, ex-Whigs, former Democrats, and Free-Soilers had come together in the North, endorsing free soil and calling themselves the Republican Party. The elements of an ultimate confrontation with the South were falling into place. Abolitionists suddenly found themselves facing a huge antislavery constituency.

By abolitionist standards, of course, this "moral revolution" in politics was partial, halfhearted, and blighted by a widespread hostility toward African Americans. As the Northern Whigs and anti-Nebraska Democrats united against the Kansas–Nebraska Act, it was again clear that white supremacy, not racial egalitarianism, informed the renewed cry for "free soil, free labor, free men." Immediatists, when judged against this standard, remained unique in their belief in racial egalitarianism. But how were abolitionists to influence and arouse this greatly expanded antislavery coalition, so laced with racism but so militant as well in resisting Southern demands? Such tactics as third parties and disunionist agitation could no longer exert even the limited influence that they had had in the 1840s. The anti-Kansas–Nebraska movement, like the broad Northern resistance to the Fugitive Slave Law, left abolitionists with little to do beyond condoning or abetting the violence that increasingly punctuated the quickening sectional conflict.

Violence aplenty lay ahead. Once passed, the Kansas–Nebraska Act provoked a footrace to the territories as free-staters and pro-slavery supporters sought to control the elections which were to decide the territories' future by popular sovereignty. In Kansas, the political struggle soon degenerated into guerrilla warfare; many abolitionists welcomed the news of frontier bloodshed. Lydia Maria Child, an exemplar of pacifism, was outraged that some free-staters had allowed themselves to be disarmed by pro-slavery authorities without a struggle. In Massachusetts, even the "gentlemen of property and standing" inched their way into the anti-Southern consensus as old-line textile merchants, led by Amos A. Lawrence, attempted to harness popular anger over events in Kansas and move it in a conservative direction. Lawrence underwrote the New England Emigrant Aid Company and the National Kansas Committee, corporations which recruited free-state settlers with offers of capital and rifles (called by some "Beecher's Bibles"), they attracted the support of the now-familiar abolitionist militants — Thomas Wentworth Higginson, Theodore Parker, Samuel Gridley Howe, and Wendell Phillips.

Once again, radical abolitionists were being caught up in broader trends of violence-laden politics. Garrisonian Charles B. Stearns, the roving reporter for both *The Liberator* and *The National Anti-Slavery Standard*, was a believer in non-resistance. Yet, when he found himself in Kansas in 1855, he decided that killing pro-slavery men was not a violation of his pacifist creed. Most telling was what happened in June 1855 when Gerrit Smith's Liberty Leaguers convened in Syracuse for their annual meeting. Though far more interested in killing than in politicking, John Brown also attended the meeting.

Smith, Frederick Douglass, and Lewis Tappan were the most prominent of the veteran abolitionists who listened as

Brown appealed for aid in his project to protect Kansas free-staters by taking up arms. Brown left the meeting with sixty dollars; thereafter, he received financial and moral support from many reformers and politicians. Garrison, struggling to shore up the effectiveness of non-resistance, dismissed the Kansas warriors as opportunists and racists. Lewis Tappan shuddered at reports of Brown's massacre of unarmed settlers at Pottawatomie Creek and suggested that Kansas needed peaceful Christian missionaries, not "Beecher's Bibles."

Tappan was an exception, as abolitionists everywhere, some reluctantly, some with ardor, supported even John Brown's vicious use of force. Immediatists had envisioned emancipation as a way to avoid race and sectional violence; now many reformers, Garrisonians and political abolitionists alike, invited such conflict. In the May 1857 meeting of the Massachusetts Anti-Slavery Society, Henry C. Wright, still claiming to be faithful to non-resistance, argued that true abolitionists should furnish arms for slave insurrections, and in this debate Wright enjoyed the full support of Wendell Phillips. "I want to accustom Massachusetts to the idea of insurrection," Phillips declared, "to the idea that every slave has the right to seize his freedom on the spot." Garrison, his mantle of non-resistance in shreds, badgered the few remaining pacifists at the meeting into silence. The cry "No Union with Slaveholders" no longer satisfied the militants; yet disunion conventions, filled with violent rhetoric and sponsored by various Garrisonians, took place in Worcester and Cleveland in 1857.

The political effect of these gatherings on other Northerners was negative, repelling antislavery moderates with their extremist tone. Henry Wilson, Charles Sumner, Joshua Giddings, and other militant Republicans publicly disavowed such violent espousals and declined invitations to attend. Yet, no matter how diminished their distinctive voice in the Northern political process had become, the abolitionists still exercised a profound influence on the white South. Slaveholders grimly noted the disunion conventions and the calls for slave insurrection, certain that they reflected the North's true intentions —which most "black Republican" senators and representatives supported in moments of private candor.

It was the white supremacist and pro-slavery policies of President Pierce and the Democratic Party which most often aroused thoughts of bloodshed in the minds of abolitionists after the passage of the Kansas–Nebraska Act. The fact that the Pierce Administration, dominated by planter interests, pursued blatantly pro-slavery policies in Kansas only made it easier for abolitionists to justify violence. After all, as Garrisonians and Liberty Leaguers noted, Benjamin Wade, Henry Wilson, and Joshua Giddings were only the most vocal of the Northern politicians who urged Kansas free-staters to take up arms against the pro-slavery edicts of Franklin Pierce.

On May 22, 1856, Wade and Wilson themselves were seen stalking the halls of Congress, handguns bulging under their coats. Earlier that day, on the floor of the Senate, a South Carolina representative, Preston S. Brooks, had beaten Charles Sumner senseless with a heavy cane, avenging his family name for "insults" uttered by Sumner in his vituperative speech on the "Crime of Kansas." Wade and Wilson muttered threats of vengeance, and even conservative Northern "gentlemen" like Edward Everett gasped at the brutality of the deed and noted that outrage at the slaveholders was now "deeper and more dangerous" than ever before. In Kansas, news of "bleeding Sumner" hastened the cycle of events that led to pro-slavery forces sacking the free-soil town of Lawrence.

Opponents of slavery, violently inclined or not, believed that the Kansas–Nebraska Act represented the opening maneuver of a sustained offensive by the planter class. While they engaged in no documented conspiracy and often found themselves deeply divided on specific issues, slaveholding politicians clearly had common interests and ends to serve. And, like all politicians, they caucused in private, giving the appearance of a deeper conspiracy. It was also evident that many slaveholders sought room for the "peculiar institution" to expand, whether westward on the plains or southward into the Caribbean basin. So, besides the Kansas–Nebraska Act, 1854 witnessed, a major effort by some Southern politicians to make foreign policy serve the ends of slavery. The seizure by Havana officials of an American merchant vessel, the *Black Warrior*, brought from planters a demand for war and Cuban annexation. William Marcy, Pierre Soulé, John Mason, and James Buchanan, diplomats subservient to Southern interests, moved to purchase Cuba from Spain. At the same time, Southern extremists, or "fire-eaters," who entertained dreams of a sprawling Central American "slaveocracy," proposed that the African slave trade, outlawed since 1808, be resumed. This would drive down slave prices, providing poor whites with the opportunity to enjoy the role of master. When William Walker, a slaveholding soldier of fortune, temporarily gained control of Nicaragua in 1855 by a *coup d'état* and revoked that nation's emancipation decrees, antislavery Northerners felt confirmed in their grim determination to arrest the momentum of the "great slave-power conspiracy."

Those who needed further confirmation of the "slave-power conspiracy" soon received it from the United States Supreme Court when it declared that slaveholding enjoyed full legal protection throughout the United States. Following the election of 1856, in which the Republican Party's first Presidential nominee, John C. Frémont, carried eleven Northern states while losing to Democrat James Buchanan, the United States Supreme Court announced its decision in the case of *Dred Scott v. Sandford*. Scott, a slave, had been taken by his owner into territory declared free by terms of the Missouri Compromise. Aided by seventy-five Northern congressmen, Scott had sued for his freedom. Speaking for a divided court, Chief Justice Roger B. Taney not only denied Scott's suit but in a set of sweeping pronouncements gave slaveowning a theoretical standing in law which pleased even the most extreme planters. The Missouri Compromise, Taney declared, was unconstitutional; Congress possessed no power to legislate the limits of slavery's expansion. In another passage Taney added the gratuitous opinion that, according to the Founding Fathers, blacks possessed no rights before the law that whites were "bound to respect." Slavery, in short, had been elevated to the status of a national institution. White supremacy had been enshrined in the nation's laws.

Horace Greeley, reform-minded editor of the New York *Tribune*, caught the essence of the resentments that more and more Northerners were sharing as these pro-slavery events followed one another in ominous succession after 1854. "Slavery," he observed, "never left the North alone nor thought of so doing":

> "Purchase Louisiana for us," said the slaveholders. "With pleasure." "Now Florida!" "Certainly." Next: "Violate your treaties with the Creeks and Cherokees; expel those tribes, so as to let us expand our plantations." "So said, so done." "Now for Texas!" "You have it." "Next a third of Mexico!" "Yours it is." "Now break the Missouri Compact and let slavery wrestle free labor for that vast region, consecrated by that Compact to Freedom!" "Very good. What next?" "Buy us Cuba!" "We have tried, but Spain refuses to sell it." "Then wrest it from her at all hazards!"

To this list, anxious Northerners now added the Dred Scott decision.

How many more demands would they be forced to satisfy,

Northern voters wondered, before this Southern colossus commanded the nation's destiny? What was to become of the Yankee vision of America as a "free society," a nation with a countryside peopled by independent, pious, sober artisans, entrepreneurs, and farmers? What other course was there but to ignore the Dred Scott decision and insist sternly that slavery's expansion be halted, here and now and forever — that the Wilmot Proviso's demand for "free soil" be proclaimed the eternal law of the land? All over the North, these were the sentiments that Whig and Democratic politicians encountered from every quarter from agitated, angry constituents. So convinced, they fled from their parties en masse.

Contemplating these portentous developments, some abolitionists remembered older tactics and experienced some hesitation. Gerrit Smith, despite his fascination with violence, recoiled at the prospect of sectional collision. By 1857, he had embarked upon a quixotic crusade, accompanied by the famous pacifist Elihu Burritt, to promote compensated emancipation. Those same years also witnessed a resurgence of revivalism and evangelical abolitionism, as seen in the rapid expansion of Lewis Tappan's American Missionary Association, which assisted blacks from Jamaica to Canada. As early as 1850, the A.M.A. maintained five missions, thirteen stations, and sixteen physicians abroad. At the same time, Garrisonians arraigned the Republican Party for its racism, conservatism, and temporizing policies, just as they had criticized Whigs, Democrats, and Free-Soilers. Veteran Liberty men like Gerrit Smith and William Goodell also engaged in the tactics of an earlier day, keeping the Liberty League alive as a separate abolitionist party dedicated to immediatism and federally legislated emancipation. In 1856 and 1860, Smith stood as the party's Presidential nominee, attracting the support of some prominent African Americans like Frederick Douglass, Jermain Loguen, and James McCune Smith, since the League at least exposed what Elizur Wright, Jr., called sarcastically "the white man's uncivil liberties."

In the end, nearly all abolitionists outside Garrison's immediate coterie voted for the Republicans. Their reservations about the party diminished further after Giddings, Chase, Seward, Wade, and other influential leaders helped to stave off more conservative elements which were attempting to make anti-Catholicism and immigrant restriction the focus of Republican concern. Among old-line Whigs especially, the issue of legislating against foreigners and Catholics seemed to offer the basis for organizing a new unionist party which might begin to modulate national discord over slavery. By 1855, a splinter political party calling itself the Know-Nothings had taken form, based on an overtly anti-Catholic, anti-foreigners platform.

Most abolitionists, like most evangelical Protestants, harbored a deep suspicion of the international Catholic hierarchy, the religion's formalistic liturgy, and the solid anti-abolitionism of the Irish immigrants. Yet they agreed with the Republican opponents of nativism that discrimination against Catholics or foreigners would constitute a fundamental violation of the free-labor individualism which lay at the heart of the party's ideology. To interject into American politics such "new and unconscionable elements of oppression," as Giddings once called them, would deflect attention from slavery, which was the "one real issue between the Republican Party and those factions who stand opposed to it." Abolitionist hesitancy about joining the antislavery consensus decreased as the Know-Nothings' popularity declined in late 1855.

The rise and fall of the Know-Nothings illustrated the growing perplexity with politics which was surfacing within abolitionism during the last years of the 1850s. While increasing numbers of immediatists coped with complicated party realignments by hesitantly supporting the Republicans, they yearned for a morally clarifying revolution. Since the late 1830s, abolitionists had been broadly divided between politics and perfectionism. But by 1859 such designations had become meaningless. Now abolitionists seemed confronted by a most intolerable choice. Either they joined the wave of Republican antislavery sentiment or they applauded violent upheaval. Most ended up attempting to do both, thanks to John Brown and Abraham Lincoln. By 1859, these two men had satisfied the abolitionists' contrary impulses to avail themselves of both ballots and bullets.

Many abolitionists were less surprised than they admitted in October 1859 upon hearing that Brown and his armed band had been foiled while raiding Harpers Ferry, Virginia, in an attempt to provoke mutiny among the slaves. Indeed, some of abolitionism's most violence-prone figures — Samuel Howe, Thomas Wentworth Higginson, Gerrit Smith, Theodore Parker, Franklin L. Sanborn, George Luther Stearns, and Frederick Douglass — had helped to finance Brown's attack. Others had known that Brown was contemplating a violent course, and Brown himself spoke openly about his plans. Black activists in Canada, such as Harriet Tubman and Jermain Loguen, as well as leaders living in the United States like Douglass, were well informed by Brown himself of what was to come.

Besides, politicians and reformers by the score — among them Joshua Giddings, Wendell Phillips, William Goodell, Henry Wilson, Charles Francis Adams, Benjamin Wade, and George W. Julian — had approved when Brown pleaded at meetings for money to support his Kansas adventures. Brown's magnetism, his skill at manipulating others, and his prophetic vision had overwhelmed these presumably responsible individuals. "Old Brown" was an immensely complex and dangerous man, endowed with a personality of immense power. He satisfied men's romantic desire to flirt with conspiracy. Openly or unconsciously, they yearned for a dramatic example of direct action, and Brown complied. After many weeks of preparation, he and his desperate band of eighteen descended on Harpers Ferry, seized the federal arsenal, and took several hostages, seeking to incite insurrection among slaves and free blacks. But the startled slaves refused to join Brown's army of liberation, and his brigade was routed by troops under Colonel Robert E. Lee's command. The raid on Harpers Ferry can perhaps be best understood, not as Brown's supreme act of will, but as a predictable result of the abolitionists' mounting desire for confrontation and their flirtation with violence after the Compromise of 1850.

Abolitionists rushed to embrace Brown's insurrectionary deeds as he was arraigned, given a semblance of a trial, then sentenced and hanged by Virginia authorities in the winter of 1859. Brown orchestrated his own martyrdom with consummate skill, issuing statements to the press and composing letters which were quickly published. New England's intellectual elite, Ralph Waldo Emerson, Henry Wadsworth Longfellow, and Henry David Thoreau, eloquently celebrated Brown's courage and moral inspiration. In Brooklyn, Wendell Phillips electrified an immense audience with his dictum that "the lesson of the hour is insurrection." Brown, Phillips declared, "has twice as much right to hang Governor Wise [of Virginia] as Governor Wise has to hang him," for Brown had acted on the highest dictates of Christian duty. Lydia Maria Child tried vainly to reconcile her non-resistance with her admiration for Brown by offering to nurse the old man in prison when he was recovering from his wounds.

Some abolitionists, Garrison included, hurried to separate their belief in the slaves' inherent right to rebel from their abhorrence of Brown's terrorism. Others organized Christian antislavery conventions which tried to reassert the primacy of moral suasion. One of these, held in Chicago five days after the Harpers Ferry raid, was interrupted by black abolitionists who offered an impassioned defense of Harpers Ferry. For nearly all black activists, Brown was an unqualified hero, whereas the whites most anxious to disassociate themselves from Brown were the leaders of the Republican Party, Abraham Lincoln among them. Hoping to end any confusion between themselves and "black abolitionism," the Republicans were prominent in organizing anti-Brown protest meetings in major cities. Lincoln explained Brown to the slaveholders as an aberration that appeared from time to time in world history—the lone, mad assassin. According to Lincoln, Brown was simply the most recent of a long succession of randomly violent "enthusiasts," whose misguided deeds led each to "little else than his own execution."

Lincoln's explanation seemed astute on first hearing, but it was fundamentally inaccurate and wholly unconvincing to an outraged planter class. Even within Lincoln's own party, men like Benjamin Wade blamed the "slave power" for the Harpers Ferry raid: Brown had been driven to seek revenge for the "oppression" his family had suffered during the Kansas border wars. Charles Sumner, though far less disposed than Wade to excuse Brown's acts, expressed his admiration for "many things in the man." Most other sectionally militant Republicans did likewise. In the face of such statements, Lincoln's reassurances to the slaveholders were unconvincing. Republican efforts at moderation notwithstanding, it was now harder than ever for planters to distinguish a Salmon P. Chase from a Wendell Phillips, or even a Frederick Douglass from an Abraham Lincoln. The slaveholders' cries against the "nigger abolitionism of the black Republicans," which increased to a shrill pitch as the 1860 elections drew near, were quite understandable. They also contained important elements of truth.

For all its unabashedly racist supporters, for all its platform promises not to meddle with slavery where it existed, for all its deafening official silence in 1860 on questions like the interstate and District of Columbia slave trades, the Republican Party incorporated a crucial element of egalitarian vision. It did so first through the participation of Benjamin Wade, Chase, Sumner, Giddings, and many others less well known who had avowed their fervent desire to hasten the end of slavery and had attempted to secure a measure of justice for African Americans in the North. The political upheavals of the 1850s had added still others to this group. If the Republican Party became dominant, it would certainly be pressed by such men to take measures against the planter class. Moreover, the party pledged in its 1860 Presidential platform to support internal improvements, a Pacific railroad, a homestead law, and a tariff. These were promises which, if implemented, would greatly augment federal power over regionalism in the nation's economic life. Clearly, ex-Democrats as well as ex-Whigs within the Republican Party had together decided by 1860 that "free soil, free labor, and free men" could not be insured unless national authority reigned over the claims of states' rights which had heretofore shielded slavery.

Wendell Phillips, who ceaselessly excoriated the Republicans for their conservatism, appreciated these facts. In 1860, on the eve of Republican victory, he declared: "I value the success of the Republican party; not so much as an instrument, but as a milestone. It shows how far we [abolitionists] have got." For the same reasons, the Colored Man's National Suffrage Convention overwhelmingly endorsed the party, although some blacks like Henry Highland Garnet and Frederick Douglass, repelled by the Republicans' racist elements, voted for Gerrit Smith instead of Abraham Lincoln.

The planter class, unlike Phillips, perceived the Republican Party as a direct instrument of abolitionism, and they did so for several good reasons. As the voting returns confirmed Lincoln's victory in 1860, slaveholders imagined what life would be like once they had begun to feel the effects of Republican executive power. No matter how often he reaffirmed his deep reservations about black equality and his abhorrence of abolitionism, it was indisputable that Lincoln regarded slavery as a moral perversion. Because of slavery, he once stated, "our republican robe is soiled, and trailed in the dust"; the institution, he declared, put the lie to all American claims of republican liberty.

Given such views, Lincoln would certainly veto any legislation which provided for the further expansion of slavery, regardless of the Dred Scott decision. In neither branch of Congress would pro-slavery strength be sufficient to override him. And Lincoln would certainly use his immense patronage to appoint "black" Republicans to federal offices throughout the slave states. The prospect of Republican appointees running the customs service in Charleston, South Carolina, or administering the post offices in Mississippi could not be tolerated. With Lincoln in the White House, the planters feared, the American Anti-Slavery Society and its scheming British partners would at last enjoy free access to the plantation. Denied the expansion it believed was necessary for survival, scorned by world opinion, and subverted from within, Southern civilization would face extinction. Secession was the only possible choice.

To the relief of all abolitionists, Lincoln rejected any and all compromise with Southern demands for the further expansion of slavery. Sworn to uphold the Union by force of arms, he called for seventy-five thousand volunteers after South Carolinian troops fired on the federal arsenal at Fort Sumter. By April 1861, whatever non-resistance or disunionism was left within abolitionism vanished almost entirely as the realities of civil war were accepted. Garrisonians and Liberty Leaguers, whites and African Americans together quoted John Quincy Adams, who once averred that treasonous insurrection by slaveholders would endow Congress and the President with the power to decree emancipation. As the troops began to march, most abolitionists discarded the last vestige of their romantic radicalism for the hard world of armed conflict and power politics. Now they turned to their last, most significant task of all. Somehow, they had to transform a civil war between two antagonistic civilizations into a revolution in race relations.

8

TRIUMPH AND TRAGEDY:
ABOLITIONISTS AND EMANCIPATION

During the last months of the Civil War, news reporter Whitelaw Reid found himself in northern Alabama as he followed the Union Army. Looking for a story, he struck up a conversation with an emancipated slave who had taken shelter in an abandoned tent near the small town of Selma. What did this fellow expect, Reid inquired, now that he was rid of his master? The black man answered with emphasis, as Reid quoted him: "I's want to be a free man, cum (and go) when I please, and nobody say nuffin' to me or order me around."

Long before Union armies invaded Alabama and other parts of the Deep South, abolitionists had begun demanding much the same things on behalf of people like the slave Reid talked to. Slavery must be destroyed and black Southerners guaranteed their full civil rights, they insisted. Only if blacks were granted full, nationally guaranteed citizenship could the carnage of warfare be justified, the "slave power" permanently dismantled, and the North purged of its white supremacist ways.

Ultimately, a South emerged which partially fulfilled yet cruelly blighted this black Alabamian's hopes for freedom and dignity. In the end, no person living in the United States would be legally able to claim another as property. In theory and for a time in practice, emancipated slaves came to enjoy full legal protection and civil rights, defined and enforced by federal power, constitutional amendments, and Acts of Congress. Abolitionists and agencies of government also worked together to secure some measure of economic security and political independence for these newly empowered citizens.

But, in the end, abolitionists and former slaves were to discover that emancipation led to sharecropping, segregation, and the terrors of white vigilantism. The black Alabamian's descendants were not to come and go as they pleased, escape white coercion, and avoid being ordered around. The South's traditions of caste oppression and rural parochialism, modified but intensified by military defeat, eventually prevailed.

As the Civil War's brutal dimension became evident, abolitionists everywhere concerned themselves with a more immediate matter closely connected with the ultimate fate of the South. Their task, quite simply, was to convince a skeptical Northern majority that ending slavery, not preserving the Union, should be the overriding goal of the war. But in the first months after the firing on Fort Sumter, it became clear that most Republicans construed the war in anything but abolitionist terms.

Immediately following the rout of the Union Army at the first battle of Bull Run in August 1861, Congress declared that the sole purpose of pursuing hostilities was "to preserve the Union, with all the dignity, equality and rights of the several states unimpaired." In the House, Thaddeus Stevens, Owen Lovejoy, and other radical Republicans offered no remonstrance as this measure passed with only two dissenting votes. *The Springfield Republican* in Illinois, widely respected as a sounding board for Lincoln's own views, expressed the mood perfectly in June 1861, observing: "If there is one point of honor upon which . . . this administration will stick, it is its pledge not to interfere with slavery in the states."

Several facts explain the Republicans' stance, which was so obviously in conflict with the abiding hatred of slavery nurtured by the party's more radical members. For one thing, Lincoln and other leaders shared a deep preoccupation with retaining the loyalty of unionist elements in Kentucky, northern Virginia, Tennessee, Maryland, Delaware, Missouri, and other border states. Of obvious military value, these middle-ground areas still maintained slavery. The whites living there defended slaveholding as a legitimate exercise of property rights and felt ill-disposed toward free blacks and abolitionists. Republicans feared that precipitous action against slavery would drive these important states from the Union cause.

Besides, even Republican radicals like Thaddeus Stevens were acutely aware that their party had captured a Northern majority precisely because it had stressed antislavery moderation. A very large bloc of race-conscious voters, especially in the Midwest, had endorsed free soil with enthusiasm, fully assured that Abraham Lincoln was in no way pledged to destroy slavery in the South, either immediately or in some distant future, and held no brief for "equalizing" the races. The 1860 Republican platform had disclaimed all such intentions, and especially during the war's early phases, the Republican coalition was complex and very fragile. The party would not be kept together if the goal of emancipation came up for debate. Even as Lincoln turned his policies toward abolition, he was constantly forced to reassure the party's conservative wing. "What I do about slavery and the colored race," he averred in 1862, "I do because it helps to save the Union; and what I forbear, I forbear because I do *not* believe it would help to save the Union."

To abolitionists, statements like Lincoln's had the familiar

ring of expediency which they had long ago come to expect
from politicians. Especially in wartime, Northern politicians,
no matter how opposed to slavery, continued to value coalition
building over divisive moral crusading. Thus, abolitionists
found themselves continuing to level their familiar criticisms of
the political order. Meetings of the American Anti-Slavery Society went on as usual, as did state and local gatherings. Speakers of national prominence like William Lloyd Garrison,
Frederick Douglass, Gerrit Smith, and Wendell Phillips would
rise to demand emancipation and to denounce the Administration. Lincoln's decision in September 1861 to revoke General
John C. Frémont's declaration of martial law, which had freed
every slave belonging to rebels in Missouri, initiated open conflict between the Republican Administration and the immediatists. Garrison, hearing of the President's action, declared that
even if Lincoln was "six feet four inches high," he was "a dwarf
in mind." Throughout the war, many abolitionists retained
their alienation from a government they deemed hostile to the
goal of racial equality.

Yet there was no mistaking the enormous changes in politics
brought on by the war. For all his caution, Abraham Lincoln
was the furthest thing imaginable from the pro-slavery Presi-
dents who had preceded him. Likewise, the Republican Party
could in no respect be mistaken for the pro-slavery Whigs and
Democrats which had dominated antebellum politics. The Republicans and their President presented the abolitionists with
a perplexing mixture of frustration and promise. Sympathetic
to colonization, Lincoln had once proposed a bill in Congress
to abolish slavery in the District of Columbia which was so
generous to masters and so unmindful of the slaves that it
aroused widespread abolitionist wrath. His courtroom defense
of a master seeking the return of a fugitive had earned him
Wendell Phillips's famous nickname: "Slave-Hound from
Illinois."

But abolitionists could only approve of the Lincoln who had stated in 1858 that the Union could not continue "half-slave, half-free." Plainly, Lincoln believed, as he said so often before the war, that the "slave power" rested upon the even more "monstrous injustice" of enslavement, which "robbed our fellow men of the just fruits of their labor," a statement no abolitionist could dispute. And reformers could only agree when Lincoln insisted that "a more perfect union" could be achieved only by applying far more broadly than ever before Jefferson's insistence that "all men are created equal." No less a man than Frederick Douglass testified that he always "remained impressed with {Lincoln's} entire freedom from popular prejudice against the black race" when dealing with African Americans on a personal basis. Like his party, Lincoln embodied an expansive political vision muted by narrow expedience, and a racial egalitarianism offset by bigotry. For all their efforts to retain their independence, most abolitionists found themselves drawn by this tantalizing mixture of promise and limitation into supporting Republican candidates and applauding the party's radical wing.

Their sudden popularity among an increasing majority of Northerners also caused veteran abolitionists to ease their combative stance. As emancipation gained support in the North, editors and politicians no longer dismissed abolitionists as wild extremists but instead began to laud them as noble prophets whose warnings had proven true. While their growing prestige in no way diminished their desire to confront conventional values, the new status of abolitionists as vindicated heroes made a spirit of iconoclasm all the harder to maintain. Wendell Phillips, Gerrit Smith, and Frederick Douglass headed an impressive list of abolitionists who accepted invitations to speak in the nation's capital. Phillips's visit and private interview with Lincoln prompted the New York *Tribune*'s Washington correspondent to observe that "a year ago [he] would have been sacrificed to the Devil of Slavery anywhere on Pennsylvania Avenue." Now "he was introduced by Mr. Sumner on the floor of the Senate . . . The attentions of the Senator to the apostle of Abolition were of the most flattering character."

Phillips, who defined himself wholly by his radical commitments, now found himself in a perplexing situation that other leading abolitionists shared. By 1863, he had become the North's most sought-after public speaker, and he now reached audiences of unprecedented size. This approving Northern public now regarded him as a sage, a pundit, or an icon of popular culture, not a combative radical agitator. Though he resisted this homogenization by adopting radical positions on Southern reconstruction, many other white abolitionists were now congratulating themselves on their vindication. "Events have so changed the position of affairs that our old-time policies are no longer applicable," reported a former Garrisonian in late 1861. The sharp oppositionist posture that most abolitionists had cultivated was beginning to soften.

Nevertheless, abolitionists of both races still labored mightily to ensure that the public adopted emancipation out of moral conviction, not military expediency. Exploiting their newfound fashionability, they once again applied time-honored techniques of moral suasion, publishing newspapers, organizing rallies, and stimulating petition campaigns. In May of 1862, Sidney Howard Gay, for years the zealous Garrisonian press chief of *The National Anti-Slavery Standard*, became managing editor of Horace Greeley's august New York *Tribune*. In that same year, the New York *Independent*, underwritten by (who else?) Lewis Tappan, was entrusted to the brilliant editorial care of fervent abolitionist Theodore Tilden, who, with co-editor Henry Ward Beecher, turned the paper into a powerful emancipationist organ. As in the antebellum era, when political abolitionists cooperated with the Free-Soilers, these editors applauded the various antislavery measures which Republicans enacted in 1862. During that year, Congress approved and Lincoln signed measures for compensated emancipation in the District of Columbia, passed the Wilmot Proviso, and took steps to suppress the African slave trade.

Garrison, Gerrit Smith, and other prominent leaders tried to apply their old technique of holding rallies and conventions to the new cause of military emancipation. Together with Phillips, Edmund Quincy, Samuel Gridley Howe, and other radical Republicans, they organized Emancipation Leagues to oversee a major effort of moral susasion against conservative war aims. The League's Washington Chapter kept that city politically agitated by sponsoring a series of abolitionist speakers at the Smithsonian Institution. Lincoln was seen in the audience more than once. The Massachusetts League, directed by Samuel Sewall, a charter member of the American Anti-Slavery Society, published nearly one hundred thousand emancipationist pamphlets in 1862 alone. The Leagues also undertook a large-scale petition campaign reminiscent of the 1830s. By mid-1862, petitions bearing thousands of signatures were flooding Washington. Through such activities, abolitionists made up the vanguard of the drive for emancipation.

But these abolitionists, for all their strenuous activity, were not primarily responsible for the mounting tide of emancipation feeling. They capitalized on it, organized it, and channeled it into politics, but their moral suasion did not create it. It was the Union armies and the generals who led them, together with African American activists in the North and South, who turned emancipation from a hope into an imperative. Popular demands for emancipation stemmed at first from failures by commanders in the field. When Union generals like George B. McClellan suffered major military losses or engaged in skirmishes to no apparent purpose with the Confederate forces, leading Republicans expressed their frustration by demanding a more comprehensive assault on the South. Then it became even more obvious to most Republicans that in this terrible bloodletting the "slave power" was proving even more formidable than it had been in politics. Slowly it became clear that abolitionists and radical Republicans had a point when warning that the fundamental issues raised by the war could be resolved only by abolishing slavery. Even to those who felt deep antipathy to African Americans it became evident that restoring "the union as it was" and readmitting the planter aristocracy into the councils of the Republic would be to reawaken the fundamental conflicts over slave expansion, secession, nullification, civil liberties, violence, homestead laws, banks, tariffs, and internal improvements which had for so long divided the nation. Political necessity, if not moral obligation, now dictated emancipation. The logic of wartime politics far more than moral suasion was now making converts to the goal of abolition.

No less influential than generals and congressmen in promoting this shift of opinion were African American activists on both sides of the battle lines. In the North, blacks first agitated to be allowed to enlist in the army, and once they were accepted, they fought with great distinction, though they were paid significantly less than whites until the last months of the war and were heavily discriminated against by their white commanders. Viewing military participation as the most practical abolitionism of all, Frederick Douglass issued the pamphlet *Men of Color, to Arms!*, which exhorted potential black soldiers with the thought that "liberty won by white men would lack half its lustre. [They] who would free themselves must strike the blow . . . Action! action! not criticism is the plain duty of this hour." By mid-1863, African American troops were enlisting in regiments in Massachusetts, Ohio, Pennsylvania, and New York, and white abolitionists, especially Phillips, George Stearns, and Thomas Wentworth Higginson, played recruiting roles in the military. But the Northern black soldiers, not their white sympathizers, offered the more eloquent testimony as to the justice of ending slavery.

In the end, however, it was not abolitionists of either race or even African American soldiers, but the bondspeople themselves whose actions hastened slavery's destruction. Many slaves found themselves involved directly in the Confederate war effort, building bridges, digging trenches, excavating breastworks, and hauling supplies. Abolitionists and radical Republicans took note of these labors and argued that, since slaves were being employed so extensively by the Southern war machine, abolition constituted a military as well as a moral imperative. Other bondspeople chose a course of action which was of even greater influence on Northern opinion. As Union armies occupied coastal areas of the Deep South and carried out maneuvers in the border states, slaves by the thousands deserted their masters and sought the protection of federal authorities. Thousands more discovered that their masters had fled, and they, too, placed themselves under the Union flag — thus presenting federal authorities with bedeviling problems intimately related to emancipation.

Initially, military authorities had no grounds to regard the escapees as freed. Until mid-1862, even the Confiscation Acts passed by Congress allowing the seizure of rebel property were ambiguous regarding the disposition of slaves. This very ambiguity raised troubling questions. What standing did such persons enjoy before civil magistrates and in the eyes of criminal law? Could their rebel masters rightfully reclaim them as property? Should federal authorities return escapees to the enemy? Or should the escapees be considered spoils of war, slaves held by Yankees instead of slaves held by secessionists? Or were they in fact men and women who deserved legal protection and civil rights? These refugees from slavery forced Northerners to ponder the meaning of emancipation in the most direct and intractable terms.

But no matter what conclusions federal officials reached, their subsequent policies regarding the escapees generated support for emancipation. Democratic General George B. McClellan, no antislavery man, decided during 1861 and 1862 to return slaves to the enemy under a flag of truce. Lincoln, who initially opposed the use of military means to commandeer the slaves of rebel planters, had overridden General Frémont's attempts to do so in Missouri. But Lincoln's policy, like McClellan's, only heightened the demand for emancipation, provoking the charge that even the President and his generals were falling victims to the "slave-power conspiracy."

Unlike the pro-slavery McClellan, Generals Benjamin F. Butler, Nathaniel Banks, and Rufus Saxon designated black refugees in the coastal areas of Virginia and the Deep South as "contraband of war," a vague term that connoted neither slavery nor freedom. This eventually permitted Union generals to conscript thousands of ex-slaves into their armies as full soldiers or as noncombatants. Higginson, who took command of a "contraband" army in the South Carolina Sea Islands district in 1862, understood clearly the significance of this new policy, calling it "the most important fact in the solution of this whole Negro question."

There was merit in this assessment, as Lincoln's own rapidly evolving opinions on the fighting skills of African Americans clearly demonstrated. At first he felt that using blacks as combatants would "produce more evil than good," but by January 1, 1863, he had publicly reversed his position. His Emancipation Proclamation, issued on that date, called for recruiting "contrabands" into the army as freedmen, and these African American regiments were often more effective on the battlefield than their white counterparts. As "contrabands" and Northern free blacks dueled with the "slave power" with muskets and pikes, Northerners found the continued denial of emancipation increasingly difficult to accept. So it was that the elimination of slavery was begun on the battlefields by African American soldiers and then ratified in the Emancipation Proclamation. In this restricted but essential respect, abolition was first achieved neither by Republican politicians nor by white abolitionists but by black men and women, free and slave, who became part of a white people's civil war.

Impelled by all these pressures for emancipation, Lincoln announced in September 1862 that the "War for Union" must be transformed into a war to exterminate slavery. He still proceeded with caution, and abolitionists quickly attacked his preliminary Emancipation Proclamation as being far too limited and tainted with expedience. Lincoln hoped that his Proclamation would foster division among Confederates, stimulating "reunion" movements in the upper South and panic in the "cotton kingdom." Foreign powers, he further expected, might feel less inclined to aid the Confederacy if the North was pledged to the holy cause of eradicating slavery. For all these reasons, his new policy subjected the goal of emancipation to several important qualifiers.

Critics pointed out that the Proclamation abolished slavery only in the still-independent Confederacy, where federal law exercised no practical power. In the unionist border areas, slavery not only remained untouched but was sustained by the 1850 Fugitive Slave Law until its repeal by Congress in mid-1864. Many abolitionists, scanning the Proclamation, were distressed to find no mention of guarantees for the freedpeople's civil rights, nor provisions to prevent emancipation from leading directly to a new era of less formal but no less oppressive servitude.

Stephen S. Foster, Parker Pillsbury, Wendell Phillips, and other radical abolitionists were not alone in deploring these weaknesses. Salmon P. Chase, now Secretary of the Treasury, complained, as did many radical Republicans, that the document did not formally guarantee emancipation's permanence;

freedpeople, he feared, might well be subject to reenslavement in the future. Less radical Republicans entertained similar reservations. Lyman Trumbull, a moderate senator from Illinois, observed after reading the Proclamation that only a constitutional amendment could "insure that no state or Congress could ever restore slavery." Moreover, as abolitionists were fully aware, Lincoln had appended to this preliminary Proclamation a message in which he again proposed colonization for freedpeople and compensation for slaveowners. True, in the Emancipation Proclamation of New Year's Day 1863, the references to colonization were deleted. But Lincoln continued to stress that the Proclamation represented an act of necessity, not of morality, dictated by military and political considerations. "The President can do nothing for *freedom* in a direct manner, but only by circumlocution and delay," Garrison complained. Douglass, years later, characterized Lincoln's approach even more negatively:

> He was ready and willing at any time . . . to deny, postpone and sacrifice the rights of humanity in the colored people to promote the welfare of the white people . . . In all his education and feeling, he was an American of the Americans . . . We are at best only his step-children . . . The Union was to him more than our freedom or our future.

There was much to be said for these criticisms. Lincoln's endorsement of emancipation as a military necessity did represent a major threat to the abolitionist's cherished hopes of "moral revolution." Lydia Maria Child had exclaimed in early 1862 that "everything *must* go wrong if there is no [change of] heart or conscience," if the slaves were granted emancipation "merely as a 'war necessity.'" For over three decades, abolitionists of both races had struggled as best they knew how to eradicate white racism. They had expressed active concern for the rights of free African Americans and had long made clear their belief that the slaves, once freed, should be guaranteed legal protection and civil justice. But even as the President proclaimed emancipation, "moral revolution" remained as distant as it had been in the 1830s. Most who cheered Lincoln's Proclamations saw them as a means to punish the arrogant slaveholders by installing free-labor communities where plantations had held sway and to cripple the Confederate war effort.

Fully aware of all these problems, African American abolitionists nevertheless acclaimed Lincoln's announcement, and their white colleagues joined them enthusiastically. On New Year's Day 1863, representatives of the two abolitionisms mingled with ease at a gala celebration in New York City, hailing the promulgation of slave emancipation. For all its shortcomings, practical-minded observers properly regarded the Emancipation Proclamation as an irrevocable step toward freedom. Once the Proclamation was announced, the chances became practically nil that the more than three million black people would ever again be legally treated as property. From that time on, the Union Army would march through the rebellious states automatically emancipating slaves as it went.

African Americans could now reasonably expect to confront a new political order, probably no less racist, but one which would no longer give preponderance to a small group of Southern exploiters. Perhaps these considerations were what prompted the usually skeptical Douglass to exclaim in February 1863 that the Emancipation Proclamation constituted "the greatest event in our nation's history." Certainly, Douglass was aware that the cheers which accompanied emancipation most often echoed hatred of slaveholders instead of concern for the interests of African Americans. But the freedmen's future seemed, at last, to be an open question, one perhaps susceptible to solutions that included full citizenship, not just the absence of ownership by white masters.

Fulfilling as Lincoln's proclamation was for white abolitionists, few understood it as definitively eliminating the practice of slaveholding. Well aware that the goals of their thirty-year crusade would not be fully achieved until the Constitution itself was altered to insure permanent emancipation, abolitionists now began campaigning for the enactment of a Thirteenth Amendment. As they circulated petitions, went on lecture tours, and organized rallies, these onetime extremists found themselves working more comfortably than ever within the mainstream of Republican Party politics. Even the most conservative Republicans agreed that slavery must be expunged from the nation's laws, and they assured their constituents that abolishing slavery would in no way alter the nation as preeminently a white man's country. White supremacy in the North, they pointed out, had not been subverted by emancipation in the 1790s; segregation and discrimination had long ago proven their effectiveness in maintaining black subordination. Why should anyone fear a different result in 1865? Yet as abolitionists attempted to rebut these racist claims there was no suitable equivalent to the old Liberty Party or the anachronistic cry of "No Union with Slaveholders," no similar tool with which abolitionists could hurl defiance at the claims of racist politics.

Failing to find such a device, Wendell Phillips, Parker Pillsbury, Steven and Abby Kelley Foster, and others broke with the main body of abolitionists and denounced Lincoln's leadership. Uniting with a small group of radical Republicans, they organized a dissident convention in Cleveland to nominate John C. Frémont in Lincoln's stead as the Republican Presidential candidate in the elections of 1864. The result was not a serious challenge to the Republican Party or to the fundamental flaws of Yankee political culture, but instead a round of bitter squabbles between the pro-Lincoln Garrison and the anti-Lincoln Phillips which soon preoccupied all of abolitionism's national leadership, black and white alike. In this manner, divisive political partisanship made permanent inroads within the American Anti-Slavery Society. Yet nearly all abolitionists rejoiced when Lincoln was reelected, and nearly all praised the wisdom of his leadership when on April 9, 1865, Lee formally surrendered at Appomattox. The news of Lincoln's assassination five days later left veteran abolitionists as stunned and genuinely bereaved as all other devoted Northerners.

Then, on December 29, 1865, just after the Thirteenth Amendment was finally ratified, Garrison shocked many of his colleagues by declaring that the abolitionists' mission had ended. As Phillips and others issued torrents of protest, Garrison terminated publication of *The Liberator* forever and announced that since slavery had finally been abolished, the antislavery societies no longer served any useful purpose. Abolitionists, he advised, should either work individually to assist African Americans or join with the many recently established groups that sponsored projects to aid the newly freed slaves. By 1866, Garrison, Phillips, and their lawyers were in court to determine whether a cash bequest from an old abolitionist should be used for freedmen's aid or for subsidizing the publications of the American Anti-Slavery Society. As the South sued for peace and the Reconstruction era opened, the abolitionist movement was fragmenting, having exhausted both its powers of agitation and its capabilities as a coherently radical enterprise.

In Garrison's case, an overpowering personal need to savor public vindication had overwhelmed his resolve to continue with "the cause." The crowds of freedpeople who had greeted him during a visit to Charleston, South Carolina, had proclaimed him their "liberator," singing hymns of jubilation as they carried him triumphantly on their shoulders around the city square. The Republican Party's national nominating convention had featured him as a highly honored guest, greeting his name with loud "Huzzas!" What more assurance of the success of one's lifelong crusade could one ask for? Phillips, by contrast, remained wholly preoccupied with a political struggle for equality which he felt must be continued. Equal citizenship, he argued, remained a goal toward which radicals must ever struggle. These two towering figures, Phillips and Garrison, had now assumed diametrically opposite positions as to the meaning of emancipation, and abolitionists gravitated to the one or the other.

While Phillips, Pillsbury, Foster, Douglass, Remond, and their handful of followers tried throughout the 1860s to extend their radical roles, most abolitionists followed Garrison in making their easy peace with the post-emancipation world. The rigors of war had prepared the abolitionists for this adjustment by fostering a new sense of practicality. After 1861, the pressures to mobilize militarily, to close ranks politically, and to enforce military discipline even on the "home front" had led many reformers toward a far less romantic approach to social reform which stressed incremental solutions, even to the problem of Southern reconstruction.

For this reason, those abolitionists who terminated their affiliations with the antislavery societies did not believe that they were retiring entirely from the field. They saw themselves as shifting their priorities to meet the demands of a new time. Long-standing Garrisonian J. Miller McKim best captured the essence of this feeling when he stated that "iconoclasm has had its day" and that the "old antislavery routine" of agitating was now passé. "For the battering-ram we must substitute the hod and trowel," he advised, for "we have passed through the pulling down stage of our movement; the *building up* . . . remains to be accomplished." With slavery facing permanent extinction, many abolitionists turned eagerly to the step-by-step task of aiding the freedpeople.

Even during the war, practical-minded abolitionists like McKim had begun projects to aid the black Southerner's transition from slavery. In late 1861, Union forces seized the Sea Islands, including the town of Port Royal, off the South Carolina coast. The planters fled, leaving behind nearly ten thousand slaves and perhaps the richest alluvial lands in the nation for growing long-staple cotton and rice. For one last time, Lewis Tappan gathered together veteran abolitionists and New England philanthropists, and they, along with Salmon Chase in the Treasury Department, helped to underwrite the doctors, teachers, labor superintendents, and supplies that were streaming into the Sea Islands by mid-1862. The "Gideonites," as the biblically minded Port Royal abolitionists called themselves, established schools in which freedpeople learned eagerly and easily. Freedom, everyone knew, required scrutinizing labor contracts and land deeds, evaluating politicians' promises and calculating wages, prices, and interest rates; teachers and students had reason aplenty for taking their tasks very seriously.

In the South Carolina cotton fields and rice plantations, freedpeople worked with industry and innovation as free laborers, ofttimes organizing collectively to ward off exploitation by white landowners. For all its tribulations with government bureaus and its overtones of white paternalism, the Port Royal experiment indicated from the first that recently enslaved people were fully able to maintain productive communities run by vigilant citizens, so long as they were provided with three things: political support, military protection, and material assistance.

Abolitionists, however, could furnish only the last of these prerequisites. Throughout Reconstruction, the power to provide political support and military protection resided almost exclusively with the Republican majority in Congress. The several thousand teachers, philanthropists, and political organizers who traveled South, and indeed the freedpeople themselves, were acutely aware of the importance of decisions made by politicians in Washington. So were the many abolitionist leaders like Garrison, Whittier, Smith, Phillips, Weld, Chapman, the Stantons, and Child who were now administering Education Societies and Freedmen's Aid Commissions to solicit both funds and recruits for Southern projects.

Early 1865 found many of these individuals, including a contingent of the most prominent black abolitionists, lobbying openly in Washington for the expansion of the Freedmen's Bureau, a federal agency created at the close of the war to assist the resettlement of emancipated slaves. Chartered by Congress in 1865 after three years of lobbying by abolitionists, the Freedmen's Bureau quickly became essential to Yankee efforts to remake Southern society. The Bureau's appropriations underwrote school construction, paid the moving expenses of Northern teachers, and supplied books and equipment.

By 1866, however, some abolitionists had concluded that even direct intervention could not truly guarantee the freedmen's fundamental liberties. Wendell Phillips Garrison, son of the "original liberator," expressed feelings that were beginning to enjoy support among the most radical abolitionists and Republicans. "To free the slave, and then abandon him in an anomalous position betwixt bondage and manhood," was as cruel as enslavement itself, he wrote. Calling for the total reorganization of Southern society, he demanded that the federal government develop a policy of "absolute justice" designed to guarantee no less than full citizenship for the former slaves. The reconstruction of the South must be "thorough," he stressed, "and affect its constitutions, statutes and customs."

For the abolitionists who stood with Wendell Phillips, it seemed that the program now required the federal government to exercise a wholly unprecedented array of national powers. It must confiscate the vast tracts belonging to rebel planters and redistribute them in forty-acre allotments to the former slaves. Retributive justice as well as the dictates of philanthropy could be satisfied, they argued, only if the freedmen were compensated for the generations of exploitation they and their forebears had endured. Besides, as abolitionists like young Garrison were well aware, equality for African Americans in the South and in the nation as a whole would have permanence only if the freedpeople controlled a significant share of the region's economic resources. Otherwise, blacks might enjoy the theoretical guarantees of equal legal protection and even vote in every election, yet still remain powerless before their vengeful white neighbors.

With their demands for the education of freedmen and for black equality in civil rights, the abolitionists both culminated and terminated their historic crusade. Their attempts to obliterate race hierarchy and restructure class position in the old slave states seemed in some ways to have brought them full circle, and were reminiscent of their efforts in the North before the war. "Gideonite" teachers instructing black children in the Carolina Sea Islands certainly harked back to Prudence Crandall's protracted struggles in the 1830s to open her girls' school to black children. Abolitionist demands that Congress guarantee the freedpeople's civil rights recalled the days when they had petitioned state legislators and filed suits to end disenfranchisement in the North. Their insistence on land redistribution and black economic uplift in the South had likewise been prefigured in the white abolitionists' early sponsorship of manual-labor academies for Northern African Americans and in Gerrit Smith's attempts to found black free-labor colonies on his estates. For decades, abolitionists of both races had sought by such means to demonstrate to racist disbelievers the capacity of oppressed people to become full and productive citizens.

Now, on a much expanded scale, the Port Royal experiment, the work of the Freedmen's Bureau, and the efforts in Congress to obtain guarantees of black enfranchisement offered much the same prospect.

Wendell Phillips accurately glimpsed even more profound continuities which linked the abolitionists' final drive for a radical Southern reconstruction to the turbulent antebellum decades. The Civil War, he said, was not just a struggle arising from disagreements over slavery, party platforms, and the nature of the Union. It was, to be sure, made up of all these things, but it was much more — an ultimate collision of two irreconcilable cultures. "What is the history of our seventy years?" he asked audiences on the eve of the Union victory. "It is the history of two civilizations constantly struggling, and always at odds, *except when one or the other rules.*"

The North, he stated, exemplified "the civilization of the nineteenth century" with its complete adherence to the "equal and recognized manhood" of "free labor, free speech, open Bibles, the welcome rule of the majority [and] the Declaration of Independence." The South, in entire antithesis, contained anachronisms which recalled "the days of Queen Mary and the Inquisition." It was an "aristocracy of the skin," intolerant of free inquiry, hostile to self-rule, wedded to "violence," blighted by "ignorance," mired in "idleness," and dedicated to the axiom that "one third of the race is born booted and spurred, the other two thirds ready for that third to ride."

The war's deepest meaning, Phillips emphasized, could be understood only if seen as part of a much longer struggle for a common republican nationality in America. True peace could be achieved, therefore, not by signing treaties or by enacting laws, but by "carrying Massachusetts to Carolina," by applying "Northern civilization all over the South." Every inherited privilege, every form of parochialism and patriarchy, must be uprooted from the Southern landscape. In their place, a class of independent yeomen and artisans must arise, free laborers whose productive efforts supported common schools, free churches, and democratic institutions of all sorts. "We must take up the South and organize it anew," Phillips urged, "to absorb six millions of ignorant, embittered, bedeviled Southerners [black and white] and transmute them into honest, decent, educated Christian mechanics, worthy to be brothers of New England Yankees."

Expressed with the eloquence and redoubled force of finality, Phillips had invoked the vision which in some way had shaped every facet of the North's long crusade against slavery. As abolitionists hurried south, they spoke of "planting the Northern pine" in the Southern cotton fields. This phrase expressed their intention to follow Phillips's advice, to eradicate race inequality and provincial "ignorance" with the leveling codes of the Bible, the McGuffey Reader, and the honest contract between laborer and employer. Long before, back in Boston in 1833, the signers of the Declaration of Sentiments of the American Anti-Slavery Society had entertained identical hopes for a South of the future. Now, for a brief period in the mid-1860s, as they demanded ballots, land, education, and direct governmental protection for the freedpeople, these abolitionists glimpsed the tantalizing prospect of ultimate success.

But the initiative in shaping Reconstruction lay not with the abolitionists but with the Republican Congress. Here, for a time, reformers saw great cause for hope. Within the party's initially small but clearly abolitionist wing, senators and representatives such as Charles Sumner, Benjamin Wade, Thaddeus Stevens, George W. Julian, and Owen Lovejoy openly shared the old immediatists' desire to remake Southern society by guaranteeing the civil equality of its African American population. Then, by 1866 and 1867, the pro-Southern policies of Lincoln's successor, Andrew Johnson, together with the recalcitrance of the defeated Confederates, had driven a huge bloc of moderate and even conservative Republicans to join the radical wing in insisting on a stringent Reconstruction program.

Johnson's pardoning of prominent rebels, his approval of state-enacted "black codes" which were highly prejudicial to the freedpeople, his veto of the bill extending the Freedmen's Bureau's life, and, above all, his insistence that Reconstruction policy lay entirely within his Presidential prerogative, made Republicans in Congress suddenly fear that they had won the war only to lose the peace. The "slave power," it seemed, remained as actively conspiratorial as ever, now invading the offices of the Chief Executive, contriving to reestablish slavery in all but name, and working toward the overthrow of the Republican Party. Once again, and for the last time, an antislavery consensus established itself as a majority in politics; egalitarianism and political calculation once again supported each other as Congress enacted legislation designed to ensure that freedpeople would retain full citizenship.

Abolitionists' highest expectations for radical Reconstruction were destined for disappointment. For all the single-mindedness of the Sumners and Stevenses, Republican efforts to combat Andrew Johnson were no more a sign of a fundamental shift in the nation's racial attitudes than was most opposition to the "slave power" touched off in 1854 by the Kansas–Nebraska Act. "Moral revolution" remained as elusive as ever. As rank-and-file Republican voters went to the polls in the later 1860s, many of their representatives evinced racist motives when urging their constituents to vote for the Fourteenth and Fifteenth Amendments. Though designed explicitly to uphold the rights of the freedpeople in the South and African Americans everywhere, such measures, some leading Republicans claimed, would assure the freedpeople's contentment with their lives and lessen the threat of a massive black exodus to the North. In many areas, especially in urban centers and in regions close to the Southern border states, racist Northern opinion arrayed itself directly against the Republicans' Southern policies.

No matter how democratic his private views might be, no Republican Party leader could avoid being influenced by racism in the electorate. Extensive land confiscations and redistribution to the freedpeople proved too sweeping a plan, especially when a racist outlook was complemented by the Republicans' broad commitment to the right of private property. In late 1865, when Andrew Johnson returned to their original owners most of the lands already distributed to freedmen, only a few Republicans made serious remonstrances. Abolitionists who shared William Lloyd Garrison's opinions on Reconstruction also adopted a wary posture toward expanding the federal government's power in the South. Their own long-standing belief in the efficacy of individual initiative led many to oppose confiscation and to declare that the freedmen must "elevate themselves" by their own efforts.

In other respects, too, radical Reconstruction was characterized not by severity but by mildness and brevity. In several of the old Confederate states such as Virginia, the period of federally supported radical rule lasted less than a year. Border states like Tennessee and Maryland experienced hardly any Reconstruction at all, and throughout the South the federal forces deployed to uphold black civil rights were usually minimal. Even the radical Republicans were far more moderate and willing to compromise than had once been supposed. Up to the very end of the era, into the late 1870s and 1880s, those abolitionists who remained at all vocal found themselves protesting the majority's racial prejudices and the moral negligence of politicians.

Once the rebel states had complied with the Republicans' congressional demands and had been readmitted to the Union, what could abolitionists do to further ensure the freedom of the South's black citizens? Some continued to lobby for legislation like the Civil Rights Act that Charles Sumner sponsored in the twilight of his career, in 1874 and 1875. Others tried to keep the Republican Party mindful of its antislavery principles by opposing the efforts of "liberal" Republicans in 1872 to turn the party to other issues. Some abolitionist veterans took care to inculcate in their children the traditions of the movement, a fact which explains why so many of them were to be found decades later underwriting African American educational institutions in the South and supporting nascent civil-rights groups in the North. Atlanta, Fisk, and Howard universities as well as Talladega, Spelman, and Tougaloo colleges were founded with abolitionist help. During the 1870s, moreover, a young W. E. B. Du Bois was discovering models for his own luminous career in Frederick Douglass, Martin Delany, and Wendell Phillips. Abolitionism's legacy for civil rights and black liberation was confirmed even as the movement was consigned to history.

The Republican commitment to African American people, always tenuous, soon wavered and finally collapsed. Radical Republicans retired, were voted out of office, or went on to espouse other causes. In their place came "Gilded Age" politicians and civil-service reformers, men who spoke for powerful constituencies which hardly perceived racial democracy as synonymous with national, sectional, or class interest. Following the elections of 1876, when the Southern states again assumed control of their racial affairs, abolitionists protested strongly. Those citizens who nodded in agreement nevertheless felt no compulsion to act, and without motivated constituents, abolitionism amounted only to a series of moral assertions, not a compelling call to action.

Little wonder that many immediatists who still yearned for social change embraced other causes—Phillips adopted labor reform, women's rights, municipal reform, and a host of other movements. Lysander Spooner explored libertarianism, while Elizur Wright, Jr., revolutionized the life-insurance industry by inventing actuarial tables and also became an atheist. Susan B. Anthony, Elizabeth Cady Stanton, and Lucretia Mott carried the feminist-abolitionist tradition forward into an extended postbellum drive for women's rights. Many of these women and a number of male abolitionists also took on the task of eliminating prostitution in the cities and "improving" the morals of a new wave of immigrants.

All the while, Southern African Americans made their way in a new world, a world without slavery. True, it was a world ruled by hostile whites. Some were powerful planters who still commanded massive numbers of African American laborers as sharecroppers. Others delighted in lynch mobs. Civil-rights laws and access to the franchise often meant little, but sometimes they could signify much, as the blacks who participated in the Farmers' Alliances of the 1880s and the Populist revolt of the 1890s demonstrated. Most important, in this new South there was no legal buying and selling of people, no constant, crippling threat of personal disruption which had so deeply blighted the world of the slaves. Here, at least, was something of what the black refugee had meant when he told Whitelaw Reid of his wish to be a free man and to come and go as he pleased. In retrospect, the differences between formal enslavement and systematic exploitation of sharecroppers might seem small. In light of testimony taken during the 1930s from former slaves who survived both eras, however, such was hardly the case.

In the final analysis, abolitionists could not persuasively claim that their thirty-year movement had led directly to the destruction of slavery, and some even admitted that theirs had been, at best, an ambiguous victory. Generals Sherman and Grant, not Garrisonians and Liberty men; warfare between irreconcilable cultures, not moral suasion, had intervened between master and slave. Emancipation left America not clothed in righteousness but reconfirmed in white supremacism. Frederick Douglass, who well understood these things, took final stock of the abolitionist movement this way: "Liberty came to the freedmen . . . not in mercy, but in wrath, not by moral choice, but by military necessity, not by the generous action of the people among whom they were to live . . . but by strangers, foreigners, invaders, trespassers, aliens and enemies." Abolitionists, in short, remained bound by the limits of their age. As Douglass said: "Nothing was to have been expected other than what has happened." Yet it cannot be concluded that the abolitionists failed to overcome the forces of white supremacy, or that they should have healed the ills of segregation, impoverishment, and racial hostility, which plague us still. If the inheritance of the Civil War seems dispiriting, the history of the abolitionist movement certainly need not be.

Facing adversity no less daunting than in any subsequent time, abolitionists discovered terrible truths and laid them bare before their fellow citizens. Among themselves, they nurtured rich dialogues concerning the meaning of race, gender, and equality unprecedented for their candor and inclusiveness, discussions which engaged whites with African Americans, women with men, those with wealth with those of common circumstance. These dialogues yielded sure moral judgments and empowering political insights grounded solidly in daily experience. These, in turn, led abolitionists to searching critiques of custom and government that sustained them in lifetimes of civic engagement. And, above all, abolitionists engaged the world and one another honestly, fearlessly exploring their movement's internal tensions while issuing indictments of society's deep injustices. As we face our own responsibilities of citizenship, we look with pride and hope, and also for instruction, to the legacy of these holy warriors.

BIBLIOGRAPHY

The literature on abolitionism is large and complex. The following bibliography is designed to make this literature accessible to readers while indicating its bearing on each chapter of this volume.

PREFACE: SLAVERY IN REPUBLICAN AMERICA

One good introduction to abolitionism is an analysis of the way historians have interpreted the movement. Since abolitionism has always been associated with controversial issues, it is not surprising that historians have been deeply divided in their opinions of the movement's significance. Merton Dillon, "The Abolitionists: A Century of Historiography, 1959–1969," *Journal of Southern History* (1969); Richard O. Curry and Lawrence Goodheart, "Knives in Their Heads: Passionate Self-Analysis and the Search for Identity in Recent Abolitionist Historiography," *Canadian Journal of American Studies* (1983); Lawrence J. Friedman, "Historical Topics Sometimes Run Dry: The State of Abolitionist Studies," *The Historian* (1981); and Betty Fladeland, "Revisionists vs. Abolitionists: The Historiographical Cold War of the 1930s and 1940s," *Journal of the Early Republic* (1986) provide useful analyses of recent academic opinion on these questions. There are also several general histories of abolitionism which introduce the movement. Best among them are Merton Dillon, *The Abolitionists: The Growth of a Dissenting Minority* (1973) and *Slavery Attacked: Southern Slaves and Their Allies, 1619–1865* (1990).

The abolitionists can introduce themselves in their own writings. In many libraries, microfilm copies of abolitionist newspapers are available. The memoirs of leading abolitionists have also been reprinted. Good anthologies of abolitionist writings which reproduce shorter pieces are easy to obtain, including John L. Thomas, *Slavery Attacked* (1965); Louis Ruchames, *The Abolitionists* (1964); Truman Nelson, *Documents of Upheaval, Selections from the Liberator* (1966); Herbert Aptheker, *Documentary History of the Negro People*, Vol. I (1968); and, most serviceable of all, W. H. Pease and Jane H. Pease, *The Antislavery Argument* (1965). Several collections of the letters of major abolitionists have also been published. Louis Ruchames and Walter Merrill are responsible for the *Letters of William Lloyd Garrison* (1971–83); Dwight L. Dumond edited *The Letters of James Gillespie Birney, 1831–1857* (1938); and Dumond collaborated with Gilbert Hobbs Barnes in editing *The Letters of Theodore Dwight Weld, Angelina Grimké Weld and Sarah Grimké, 1822–1844* (1941). Philip Foner edited *The Life and Writings of Frederick Douglass* (1950–55), but this pioneering anthology must be supplemented by John Blassingame et al., eds., *The Frederick Douglass Papers* (1979–89). Equally essential is Peter Ripley et al., eds., *The Black Abolitionist Papers* (1985–92) and *Witnesses for Freedom: African American Voices on Race, Slavery and Emancipation* (1993), and Dorothy Sterling, ed., *We Are Your Sisters: Black Women in the Nineteenth Century* (1984).

The abolitionists cannot be properly studied without attention to the institution they opposed. For the origins of American slavery and white racism, Winthrop Jordan, *White Over Black: American Attitudes Toward the Negro, 1550–1812* (1968) is essential; Peter Wood, *Black Majority: Negroes in South Carolina* (1975) and Mechal Sobel, *The World They Made Together (1984)* analyze the early evolution of black cultures in the colonial South, a story continued brilliantly into the nineteenth century in Eugene Genovese, *Roll Jordan Roll* (1975). This work, like Genovese's *Political Economy of Slavery* (1967), emphasizes the "pre-capitalist" features of the Southern economy and social setting within which African Americans forged a culture of their own. Kenneth Stampp, *The Peculiar Institution* (1959) remains a valuable description of slavery, while Bertram Wyatt-Brown, *Southern Honor: Ethics and Behavior in the Old South* (1982) is a wise introduction to the enduring cultural values of the region. Slavery and the development of African American culture in the North are described in Edward McManus, *Black Bondage in the North* (1970) and William D. Pierson, *Black Yankees: The Development of an Afro-American Subculture in Eighteenth-Century New England* (1988).

Finally, there are several works which set "new world" slavery and abolitionism in broader patterns of historical development and academic controversy which responsible students should not neglect. These include Thomas Bender, ed., *The Antislavery Debate: Capitalism and Abolitionism as a Problem of Historical Interpretation* (1992); C. Duncan Rice, *The Rise and Fall of Black Slavery* (1975); Stanley Elkins, *Slavery: A Problem in American Institutional and Intellectual Life* (1959); Herbert S. Klein, *African Slavery in Latin America and the Caribbean* (1986); William A. Green, *British Slave Emancipation: The Sugar Colonies and the Great Experiment 1830–1865* (1976); and David Brion Davis, *The Problem of Slavery in Western Culture* (1966).

1. ABOLITION IN THE AGE OF REVOLUTION

Two works by David Brion Davis are essential to understanding abolitionism prior to the nineteenth century: *The Problem of Slavery in the Age of Revolution, 1770–1823* (1974) and *Slavery and Human Progress* (1984). Jean R. Soderlund, *Quakers and Slavery: A Divided Spirit* (1985) is an excellent analysis; Mary S. Locke, *Antislavery in America from the Introduction of African Slaves to the Prohibition of the Slave Trade, 1619–1808* supplies myriad facts, if little else. Winthrop Jordan, *White Over Black: American Attitudes Toward the Negro, 1550–1812* (1968); Duncan J. MacLeod, *Slavery, Race and the American Revolution* (1974); Gary

B. Nash, *Race and Revolution* (1990) and *Forging Freedom: The Formation of Philadelphia's Black Community, 1760–1840* (1988); and Sylvia R. Frey, "Between Slavery and Freedom: Virginia Blacks and the American Revolution," *Journal of Southern History* (1983) address relationships between slavery and the American quest for independence. William C. Nell, *Colored Patriots of the American Revolution* (1855) is both a founding document in African American history and a revealing statement of the relationship between black abolitionist historical consciousness and the meaning of the American Revolution. The progress of Northern abolitionism in the Revolutionary era is analyzed well in James D. Essig, *The Bonds of Wickedness: American Evangelicals against Slavery, 1770–1808* (1982); Shane White, *Somewhat More Independent: The End of Slavery in New York City, 1770–1810* (1991); Arthur Zilversmit, *The First Emancipation: The Abolition of Slavery in the North* (1967); and Gary B. Nash and Jean R. Soderlund, *Freedom by Degrees: Emancipation in Pennsylvania and Its Aftermath* (1991). Benjamin Quarles, *The Negro in the American Revolution* (1961) chronicles black efforts at self-emancipation.

In Ira Berlin, *Slaves without Masters: The Free Negro in the Antebellum South* (1974), the limits of Southern antislavery are explored, along with the ever more precarious circumstances of free blacks in the post-Revolutionary South. Other works which bear on Southern slavery and antislavery during the Revolution include Jeffrey Crow, *The Black Experience in Revolutionary North Carolina* (1973); Robert McColley, *Slavery in Jeffersonian Virginia* (1964); and Edmund S. Morgan, *American Slavery and American Freedom: The Ordeal of Revolutionary Virginia* (1975).

Gerald Mullin, *Flight and Rebellion: Slave Resistance in Eighteenth Century Virginia* (1972) and Douglas Egerton, *Gabriel's Rebellion: The Virginia Slave Conspiracies of 1800 and 1802* (1993) explore the Revolution's political impact on Southern African

Americans. Barbara Jeanne Fields, *Slavery and Freedom on the Middle Ground: Maryland in the Nineteenth Century* (1985) and William W. Freehling, *The Road to Disunion: Secessionists at Bay, 1776–1854* (1990) detail the emergence and significance of the upper South as a distinct region.

The relationships of slavery, antislavery, and the politics of the Republic immediately after 1787 are explored in David Brion Davis, *The Problem of Slavery in the Age of Revolution, 1770–1823* (1974) and *Revolutions: Reflections on American Equality and Foreign Liberations* (1989); Duncan J. MacLeod, *Slavery, Race, and the American Revolution* (1974); Donald Robinson, *Slavery in the Structure of American Politics, 1765–1820* (1971); and Staughton Lynd, *Class Conflict, Slavery and the United States Constitution* (1967).

For the history of antislavery thought in the early nineteenth century, Alice D. Adams, *The Neglected Period of American Antislavery, 1808–1831* (1908) is bereft of interpretation but stuffed with facts. Phillip J. Staudenraus, *The African Colonization Movement* (1961) supersedes earlier treatments; George Fredrickson, *The Black Image in the White Mind: The Debate on Afro-American Character and Destiny, 1817–1914* (1971) puts colonization and other antebellum white efforts to "solve the Negro problem" in a broad context of racist and reform thought. Specific slavery-related political crises of the early nineteenth century are treated in Glover Moore, *The Missouri Controversy, 1819–1821* (1953) and in William W. Freehling, *Prelude to Civil War: The Nullification Crisis in South Carolina, 1816–1836* (1966), a book with a much broader focus than the title might imply. John Lofton chronicles the Denmark Vesey slave revolt in *Insurrection in South Carolina* (1964), but this work should be balanced by Richard C. Wade, "The Vesey Plot Reconsidered," *Journal of Southern History* (1964).

2. IMMEDIATE EMANCIPATION

Six essential works deal with the relationships of evangelical religion, economic change, and the rise of abolitionism: Gilbert H. Barnes, *The Antislavery Impulse, 1830–1844* (1933); Whitney Cross, *The Burnt-Over District: The Social and Intellectual History of Religious Enthusiasm in Western New York* (1950); Paul Johnson, *Shopkeepers' Millennium: Society and Revivals in Rochester, New York, 1815–1837* (1978); John Quist, *Restless Visionaries: The Social Roots of Antebellum Reform in Alabama and Michigan* (1996); Randolph A. Roth, *The Democratic Dilemma: Religion, Reform and the Social Order in the Connecticut River Valley of Vermont, 1791–1850* (1987); and Robert H. Abzug, *Cosmos Crumbling: American Reform and the Religious Imagination* (1994). Other valuable analyses include John L. Thomas, "Romantic Reform in America, 1815–1865," *American Quarterly* (1965); William G. McLaughlin, "Pietism and the American Character," *American Quarterly* (1965); David Brion Davis, "The Emergence of Immediatism in British and American Antislavery Thought," *Mississippi Valley Historical Review* (1962); and Ann C. Loveland, "Evangelicalism and Immediate Emancipation in American Antislavery Thought," *Journal of Southern History* (1966). For an eloquent example of how evangelical religiosity could be transformed into African American radicalism, see Sean Wilentz, ed., *David Walker's Appeal* (1995).

A large body of work probes the deeper sociopsychological wellsprings of the white abolitionist commitment. Unstinting sympathy with abolitionist goals leads to an excessive preoccupation with defending the white reformers' "normality" in Martin Duberman, "The Abolitionists and Psychology," *Journal of Negro History* (July 1962) and Gerald Sorin, *The New York Abolitionists: A Case Study of Political Radicalism* (1971). David Donald, "Toward a Reconsideration of the Abolitionists," in *Lincoln Reconsidered* (1956) and Leonard Richards, *"Gentlemen of*

Property and Standing": *Anti-Abolition Mobs in Jacksonian America* (1970) offer contrasting but equally challenging explanations of the young abolitionists' relationships to the "market revolution." Bertram Wyatt-Brown explores the social sources of abolitionist alienation in "Prelude to Abolitionism: Sabbatarian Politics and the Rise of the Second Party System," *Journal of American History* (1971) and "New Leftists and Abolitionists: A Comparison of American Radical Styles," *Wisconsin Magazine of History* (1970).

For an exploration of the private world of the white abolitionist and its ideology, see especially Ronald Walters, *The Antislavery Appeal: Abolitionism After 1830* (1978); Lewis Perry, " 'We Have Had Conversation in the World': The Abolitionists and Spontaneity," *Canadian Journal of American Studies* (1975); Lewis Perry and Michael Fellman, eds., *Antislavery Reconsidered: New Perspectives on the Abolitionists* (1979); and Lawrence J. Friedman, *Gregarious Saints: Self and Community in American Abolitionism, 1830–1870* (1982). Elizabeth B. Clark, " 'The Sacred Rights of the Weak': Pain, Sympathy and the Culture of Individual Rights in Antebellum America," *The Journal of American History* (1995) considers the unprecedented feelings of empathy that white abolitionists developed toward the enslaved. James Huston, "The Experiential Basis of the Northern Antislavery Impulse," *Journal of Southern History* (1990) argues persuasively that abolitionists' direct observations of slavery's cruelty and exploitation drove some of them to embrace immediatism.

Four excellent works detail the relationship of women's evolving roles, religion, and reform: Lori D. Ginsburg, *Women and the Work of Benevolence: Morality, Politics and Class in the Nineteenth Century United States* (1990); Mary Ryan, *The Cradle of the Middle Class: The Family in Oneida County, New York* (1985); Nancy A. Hewett, *Woman's Activism and Social Change: Rochester, New York, 1822–1872* (1984); Nancy Cott, *The Bonds of Wom-*

anhood: 'Woman's Sphere' in New England, 1785–1835 (1977).
Three studies suggest some of the larger cultural influences to which white abolitionists responded: David Rothmann, *The Discovery of the Asylum* (1970); Karen Halttunen, *Confidence Men and Painted Women: A Study of Middle Class Culture in America, 1830–1870* (1982); and Sean Wilentz, *Chants Democratic: New York City and the Rise of the American Working Class, 1788–1850* (1984).

The form and fate of the upper South antislavery movement can be followed in Merton Dillon, *Benjamin Lundy and the Struggle for Negro Freedom* (1966); Gordon E. Finnie, "The Antislavery Movement in the Upper South before 1840," *Journal of Southern History* (1969); and James Brewer Stewart, "Radicalism and the Evangelical Strain in Southern Antislavery Thought during the 1820s," *Journal of Southern History* (1974). William H. Freehling, *Prelude to Civil War* (1966) helps to illuminate the racial and political crises of the late 1820s and early 1830s; Richard H. Brown, "The Missouri Crisis, Slavery, and the Politics of Jacksonianism," *South Atlantic Quarterly* (1966) explains the pro-slavery direction taken by mass politics during the 1820s.

Two essential works deal with the deeper ideological and social matrices of the Whig and Democratic parties, respectively: Daniel Walker Howe, *The Political Culture of the American Whigs* (1980) and Jean Baker, *Affairs of Party: The Political Culture of Northern Democrats in the Mid-Nineteenth Century* (1983). William Cooper, *The South and the Politics of Slavery* (1978) argues that Southern participation in the two-party system was wholly predicated on a defense of slavery. Richard Carwadine, *Evangelicals and Politics in Antebellum America* (1993) is essential for understanding the larger relationship of Protestantism to pre-Civil War political culture. The effect of race violence and political conflict over slavery on the emerging abolitionist movement receives attention in James Brewer Stewart, "Politics and Ideas in Abolitionism," *South Atlantic Quarterly* (1975); Donald G.

Matthews, "The Abolitionists on Slavery: The Critique behind the Social Movement," *Journal of Southern History* (1967) and Bertram Wyatt-Brown, "Stanley Elkins' *Slavery*: The Antislavery Interpretation Reexamined," *American Quarterly* (1973) examine some of the deeper objections to slavery felt by white abolitionists.

3. MORAL SUASION

For the interplay of the tactics of moral suasion, mob violence, the postal and petition campaigns, and the struggles against the gag rule, and their impact on abolitionism in the 1830s, see James Brewer Stewart, "Peaceful Hopes and Violent Experiences: The Evolution of Radical and Reforming Abolitionism, 1831–1837," *Civil War History* (1971). The long collaboration between English and American abolitionists, black as well as white, is treated in Betty L. Fladeland, *Men and Brothers: Anglo-American Antislavery Cooperation* (1972); Richard J. M. Blackett, *Building an Antislavery Wall: Black Americans in the Atlantic Abolitionist Movement, 1830–1860* (1983); and Anthony A. Barker, *Captain Charles Stuart, Anglo-American Abolitionist* (1986).

Biographical studies of leading white immediatists of the 1830s include Jane H. and William H. Pease, *Bound with Them in Chains: A Biographical History of the Antislavery Movement* (1972); Gerda Lerner, *The Grimké Sisters from South Carolina: Rebels against Slavery* (1967); Katherine Du Pré Lumpkin, *The Emancipation of Angelina Grimké* (1974); Carolyn L. Karcher, *The First Woman of the Republic: A Cultural Biography of Lydia Maria Child* (1996); Elizabeth Griffith, *In Her Own Right: The Life of Elizabeth Cady Stanton* (1984); and Dorothy Sterling, *Ahead of Her Time: Abby Kelley and the Politics of Antislavery* (1992); John L. Thomas, *The Liberator, William Lloyd Garrison:*

A Biography (1963); James Brewer Stewart, *William Lloyd Garrison and the Challenge of Emancipation* (1992) and *Wendell Phillips: Liberty's Hero* (1986); Bertram Wyatt-Brown, *Lewis Tappan and the Evangelical War against Slavery* (1969); Betty Fladeland, *James Gillespie Birney: Slaveholder to Abolitionist* (1955); Robert H. Abzug, *Passionate Liberator: Theodore Dwight Weld and the Dilemma of Reform* (1980); Stanley Harrold, *Gamaliel Bailey and Antislavery Union* (1986); Lawrence B. Goodheart, *Abolitionist, Actuary and Atheist: Elizur Wright and the Reform Impulse* (1990); Hugh Davis, *Joshua Leavitt: Evangelical Abolitionist* (1990); Donald Yacovone, *Samuel Joseph May and the Dilemmas of the Liberal Persuasion, 1797–1871* (1991); Ralph V. Harlow, *Gerrit Smith, Philanthropist and Reformer* (1939); Merton Dillon, *Elijah P. Lovejoy, Abolitionist Editor* (1961); and Robert Meredith, *The Politics of the Universe: Edward Beecher, Abolition and Orthodoxy* (1968).

Moral-suasion projects of the 1830s receive comprehensive treatment in many of the biographies just noted. Carleton Mabee, *Black Freedom: The Nonviolent Abolitionists from 1830 to the Civil War* (1970) is the most detailed study of the subject, though Gilbert H. Barnes, *Antislavery Impulse* (1934) remains the most zestful. Prudence Crandall's struggles as an educator are recounted in Susan Strane, *"A Whole-Souled Woman"*: *Prudence Crandall and the Education of Black Women* (1990). On the postal campaign specifically, see Bertram Wyatt-Brown, "The Abolitionists' Postal Campaign of 1835," *Journal of Negro History* (1963). The South's hostile responses to moral suasion are detailed in Clement Eaton, *The Freedom of Thought Struggle in the Old South* (1940); Eugene Genovese, *The World the Slaveholders Made* (1970); and William Freehling, *Prelude to Civil War* (1966).

Northern anti-abolitionism is given an essential contextual setting in racism and violence in the following: Leon Litwack, *North of Slavery* (1960); David Roediger, *The Wages of Whiteness:*

Race and the American Working Class (1991); George Fredrickson, *Black Image* (1971); David Brion Davis, "Some Themes of Countersubversion: An Analysis of Anti-Catholic, Anti-Mormon and Anti-foreign Literature," *Mississippi Valley Historical Review* (September 1960) and "Some Ideological Functions of Prejudice in Antebellum America," *American Quarterly* (Summer 1963); and David Grimsted, "Rioting in Its Jacksonian Setting," *American Historical Review* (February 1973). Leonard Richards, *"Gentlemen of Property and Standing": Anti-Abolition Mobs in Jacksonian America* (1970) addresses the broad questions of the social status of the abolitionists and their mob opponents, mob ideology, and the collective behavior of the mobs. For an insightful analysis of the relationship of race tension, gender conflict, and mob violence, consult Jean Fagan Yellin, *Women and Sisters: The Antislavery Feminists and American Culture* (1990).

4. PERFECTIONISM AND POLITICS

The growing involvement of abolitionism with issues of economics, politics, and civil liberties is described in Russel B. Nye, *Fettered Freedom: Civil Liberties and the Slavery Controversy, 1830–1860* (1949) and Larry Gara, "Slavery and the Slave Power: A Crucial Distinction," *Civil War History* (1969). A pivotal study analyzing the process by which abolitionism became part of the broad development of a Northern free-labor ideology in politics is Eric Foner, *Free Soil, Free Labor, Free Men: The Ideology of the Republican Party Before the Civil War* (1970). Three important works elaborate further on beliefs in free-labor political economy that enriched antislavery ideology: Louis Gerteis, *Morality and Utility in American Antislavery Reform* (1987); Jonathan Glickstein, *Concepts of Free Labor in Antebellum America* (1991); and Daniel J. McInerney, *The Fortunate Heirs of Freedom: Abolition and Republican Thought* (1994). David Brion

Davis, *The Slave Power Conspiracy and the Paranoid Style* (1969) analyzes the spreading belief in political conspiracy by the forces of "free" and "slave" labor among Southerners and Yankees.

For the impact of violence, the gag-rule struggles, and the rise of political antislavery on the immediatist movement of the 1830s, the following are pertinent: James Brewer Stewart, "Peaceful Hopes and Violent Experiences: The Evolution of Radical and Reforming Abolitionism, 1831–1837," *Civil War History* (December 1971) and John Demos, "The Anti-Slavery Movement and the Problem of Violent Means," *New England Quarterly* (1964). The gag-rule struggles and the role of ex-President Adams are trenchantly presented in Leonard L. Richards, *The Life and Times of Congressman John Quincy Adams* (1991). See also James M. McPherson, "The Fight against the Gag Rule: Joshua Leavitt and the Antislavery Insurgency in the Whig Party, 1839–1842," *Journal of Negro History* (1963).

The social and regional boundaries of antislavery constituencies are treated in Leonard Richards, *"Gentlemen of Property and Standing"* (1970); Eric Foner, *Free Soil, Free Labor, Free Men* (1970); Edward Magdol, *The Antislavery Rank and File* (1986); Christopher Padgett, "Hearing the Antislavery Rank-and-File: The Wesleyan Methodist Schism of 1843," *Journal of the Early Republic* (1992); Paul Goodman, "The Manual Labor Movement and the Origins of Abolitionism," *Journal of the Early Republic* (1993); and John Quist, " 'The Great Majority of Our Subscribers are Farmers': The Michigan Abolitionist Constituency of the 1840s," *Journal of the Early Republic* (1994). See also the biographies of antislavery figures of the 1840s, cited for Chapter 5.

An influential study of the collision between Garrisonians and their opponents in the American Anti-Slavery Society during the late 1830s is Aileen Kraditor, *Means and Ends in American Abolitionism: Garrison and His Critics on Strategy and Tactics, 1834–*

1850 (1969). The ongoing involvement of women in abolitionism and in the developing debates over feminism is analyzed
in Yellin, *Women and Sisters* (1991); in several of the biographies listed for Chapter 3; and in Jean Fagan Yellin and John
Van Horn, eds., *The Abolitionist Sisterhood: Women's Political Culture in Antebellum America* (1994). Gender and family as related
to the broader abolitionist beliefs are skillfully analyzed in Ronald Walters, *The Antislavery Appeal: American Abolitionism After
1830* (1976).

5. THE POLITICS OF FREEDOM

Studies of abolitionist political tactics and their effectiveness
include Aileen Kraditor, *Means and Ends in American Abolitionism*
(1969); James Brewer Stewart, *Joshua Giddings and the Tactics
of Radical Politics* (1970) and "The Aims and Impact of Garrisonian Abolitionism, 1840–1860," *Civil War History* (September
1969); Merton Dillon, *Slavery Attacked: Southern Slaves and Their
Allies* (1990); and Howard Zinn, "Abolitionists, Freedom Riders and the Tactics of Agitation," in Martin Duberman, ed.,
The Antislavery Vanguard (1965). Stanley Harrold, *The Abolitionists and the South 1831–1861* (1995) makes a persuasive case for
the extensiveness of abolitionist efforts to take direct action
within the slave states. Richard H. Sewell, *Ballots for Freedom*
(1976) is a detailed inquiry into political abolitionism in the
1840s and 1850s; Vernon Volpe, *The Forlorn Hope of Freedom*
(1990) is the best in-depth treatment of the Liberty Party. Essays found in Alan M. Kraut, ed., *Crusaders and Compromisers:
Essays on the Relationship of the Antislavery Struggle to the Antebellum Party System* (1983) are particularly valuable in assessing
the impact of antislavery on Northern politics in the 1840s and
1850s. On the impact of slave insurrections on the politics of
the 1840s, see Howard Jones, *Mutiny on the* Amistad: *The Saga
of a Slave Revolt and Its Impact on American Abolition, Law and*

Diplomacy (1986); for the "Creole mutiny," see Stewart, *Joshua Giddings* (1970).

The interplay of abolitionism and American Protestantism during the 1840s and 1850s is studied in John McKivigan, *The War Against Proslavery Religion: Abolitionism and the Northern Churches* (1984); Donald G. Matthews, *Slavery and Methodism: A Chapter in American Morality* (1965); and Timothy L. Smith, *Revivalism and Social Reform in Mid-Nineteenth-Century America* (1957). Especially stimulating on abolitionist spirituality are Lewis Perry, *Radical Abolitionism: Anarchy and the Government of God in Antislavery Thought* (1973) and Robert Abzug, *Cosmos Crumbling* (1995).

Westward expansion, the war with Mexico, and the resulting sectional crises over slavery's expansion are best approached in Bruce Levine, *Half Slave and Half Free: The Roots of Civil War* (1993). Racist thinking in westward expansion and antislavery feeling is analyzed in Reginald Horsman, *Race and Manifest Destiny* (1990); Eugene Berwanger, *The Frontier against Slavery: Anti-Negro Prejudice and the Slavery Extension Controversy* (1967); Eric Foner, "Politics and Prejudice: The Free Soil Party and the Negro, 1849–1852," *Journal of Negro History* (1965). A broader analysis of Northern expansionist ideology is found in three works of unusual importance: Major L. Wilson, *Time, Space and Freedom: The Quest for Nationality and the Irrepressible Conflict 1815–1861* (1974); Eric Foner, *Free Soil, Free Labor, Free Men* (1970); and Richard Slotkin, *The Fatal Environment: The Myth of the Frontier in the Age of Industrialization* (1978).

The politics of the free-soil movement get extended treatment in Joseph G. Rayback, *Free Soil: The Election of 1848* (1970); Frederick J. Blue, *The Free Soilers: Third Party Politics, 1848–1854* (1973); Chaplin W. Morrison, *Democratic Politics and Sectionalism: The Wilmot Proviso Controversy* (1968); and Eric Foner, "The Wilmot Proviso Revisited," *Journal of American History* (1969).

There are many biographies of the sectional politicians who rose to prominence in the North in the 1840s. Among the most useful are Martin Duberman, *Charles Francis Adams* (1960); Frank O. Gatell, *John Gorham Palfrey and the New England Conscience* (1963); David Donald, *Charles Sumner and the Coming of the Civil War* (1960); Frederick Blue, *Charles Sumner and the Conscience of the North* (1994); Richard H. Sewell, *John P. Hale and the Politics of Abolition* (1965); Richard H. Abbott, *Cobbler in Congress: The Life of Henry Wilson* (1971); Charles B. Going, *David Wilmot, Free Soiler* (1934); Glyndon Van Deusen, *William Henry Seward* (1967); Frederick Blue, *Salmon Portland Chase: A Life in Politics* (1987). Holman Hamilton, *Prologue to Conflict: The Crisis and Compromise of 1850* (1964) is a clear, short analysis.

6. RACES, CLASSES, AND FREEDOM

The complex history of the black abolitionists, their activities, ideas, and relationships with whites is best approached through Jane H. and William H. Pease's excellent *They Who Would Be Free: Blacks' Search for Freedom, 1831–1861* (1974); Richard J. M. Blackett, *Building an Antislavery Wall* (1983); and Benjamin Quarles, *The Black Abolitionists* (1969).

Major biographies of African American abolitionists include William McFeeley, *Frederick Douglass* (1991); William Cheek and Aimee Lee Cheek, *John Mercer Langston and the Fight for Black Freedom* (1989); William Edward Farrison, *William Wells Brown: Author and Reformer* (1969); Wilson J. Moses, *Alexander Crummell: A Study of Civilization and Discontent* (1989); and Cyril Griffith, *African Dream: Martin Delany and the Emergence of Pan-African Thought* (1975). Shorter biographical treatments of note include Jane H. and William H. Pease, "The Black Militant: Henry Highland Garnet" and "The Negro Conservative: Samuel Eli Cornish," in *Bound with Them in Chains* (1972); Donald Jacobs, "David Walker, Boston Race Leader," *Essex Institute*

Historical Bulletin (1971); and Robert P. Smith, "William C. Nell, Crusading Black Abolitionist," *Journal of Negro History* (1970); and the biographical essays in Richard J. M. Blackett, *Beating Against the Barriers* (1986) and David Swift, *Black Prophets of Justice: Activist Clergy before the Civil War* (1989). Shirley J. Yee, *Black Women Abolitionists: A Study in Activism, 1828–1860* (1992) is a general survey of the role of African American women in abolitionism; Jean Fagin Yellin, *Women and Sisters* (1989) contains a revealing analysis of Harriet Jacobs and Sojourner Truth.

A considerable number of narratives by slaves are available. Among the most useful are those by Frederick Douglass, Harriet Jacobs, Austin Steward, William Wells Brown, Josiah Henson, Henry Bibb, James W. C. Pennington, and Samuel Ringgold Ward. The most important academic analyses of these narratives are William L. Andrews, *To Tell a Free Story: The First Century of Afro-American Autobiography, 1760–1865* (1986) and Charles T. Davis and Henry Louis Gates, Jr., eds., *The Slave's Narrative* (1985).

Race relations between African American and white abolitionists are examined in Leon Litwack "The Emancipation of the Negro Abolitionist," in Martin Duberman, ed., *The Antislavery Vanguard* (1965); Jane H. and William H. Pease, "Ends, Means and Attitudes: Black-White Conflict in the Antislavery Movement," *Civil War History* (1972); and in the essays in Donald Jacobs, ed., *Courage and Conscience: Black and White Abolitionists in Boston* (1993). Expressions of black nationalism are examined in Floyd J. Miller, *The Search for a Black Nationality: Black Emigration and Colonization, 1787–1863* (1975) and Victor Ullman, *Martin Delany: The Beginnings of Black Nationalism* (1971).

African American cooperation with whites in opposing discrimination is stressed in Carleton Mabee, *Black Freedom* (1970); Larry Gara's *Liberty Line: The Legend of the Underground*

Railroad (1961) documents the blacks' self-sufficiency in aiding fugitive slaves. Howard Bell, A *Survey of the Negro Convention Movement, 1830–1861* (1969) explores black self-help programs of a different sort. James and Lois Horton, *Black Bostonians: Family Life and Community Struggle in the Antebellum North* (1979); Julie Winch, *Philadelphia's Black Elite: Activism, Accommodation and the Struggle for Autonomy, 1787–1848* (1988); Gary Nash, *Forging Freedom* (1988); and David M. Katzman, *Before the Ghetto: Black Detroit in the Nineteenth Century* (1973) depict the evolution of Northern African American communities. Leon Litwack, *North of Slavery: The Negro in the Free States, 1790–1860* (1960) offers a more general description of Northern white supremacist practices. Donald Yacovone, "The Transformation of the Black Temperance Movement 1827–1854," *Journal of the Early Republic* (1988) delineates the relationship between temperance and black abolitionism.

7. ABOLITIONISTS AND THE COMING OF THE CIVIL WAR

On the interplay of Northern party loyalty and sectional ideology in the early 1850s, see Joel Silby, *The Shrine of Party: Congressional Voting Behavior, 1841–1852* (1967); Michael Holt, *The Political Crisis of the 1850s* (1978); William Gnieapp, *The Origins of the Republican Party, 1852–1856* (1987); and Tyler Anbinder, *Nativism and Slavery: The Northern Know-Nothings and the Politics of the 1850s* (1992). Regarding abolitionists' increasing willingness to employ violence, see Jeffrey Rossbach, *Ambivalent Conspirators: John Brown, the Secret Six, and a Theory of Slave Violence* (1982); Thomas Slaughter, *Bloody Dawn: The Christiana Riot and Racial Violence in the Antebellum North* (1991); and Jane H. and William H. Pease, "Confrontation and Abolition in the 1850's," *Journal of American History* (1972). The 1850 Fugitive Slave law, its enforcement, and its political implications are discussed in Stanley Campbell, *The Slavecatchers: The*

Enforcement of the Fugitive Slave Law (1968); Paul Finkelman, *An Imperfect Union: Slavery, Federalism and Comity* (1991); Robert Cover, *Justice Accused: Antislavery and the Judicial Process* (1975). A number of biographies are particularly pertinent to the political fragmentation and violence of the 1850s: Henry S. Commager, *Theodore Parker: Yankee Crusader* (1947); Tilden Edelstein, *Strange Enthusiasm: A Life of Thomas Wentworth Higginson* (1968); Harold Schwartz, *Samuel Gridley Howe* (1959); Steven Oates, *To Purge This Land with Blood: A Biography of John Brown* (1970); Richard O. Boyer, *The Legend of John Brown* (1974); Fawn Brodie, *Thaddeus Stevens, Scourge of the South* (1959); Patrick Riddleburger, *George Washington Julian, Radical Republican* (1966); Edward Magdol, *Owen Lovejoy: Abolitionist in Congress* (1967); Hans Trefousse, *Benjamin Franklin Wade: Radical Republican from Ohio* (1963); Robert W. Johannson, *Stephen A. Douglas* (1973); and Don Fehrenbacher, *Prelude to Greatness: Lincoln in the 1850s* (1962). A number of the biographies listed for Chapter 5 are also valuable for an understanding of the 1850s. Harriet Beecher Stowe and *Uncle Tom's Cabin* receive especially perceptive treatment in Joan Headrick, *Harriet Beecher Stowe* (1992); Frederick Douglass's responses to the crises of the 1850s are effectively presented in David Blight, *Frederick Douglass' Civil War: Keeping Faith in Jubilee* (1989).

For the complex history of the Kansas issue and its impact on politics, see James Rawley, *Race and Politics: "Bleeding Kansas" and the Coming of the Civil War* (1969); Ronald Takaki, *A Pro-Slavery Crusade: The Agitation to Re-open the African Slave Trade* (1970) analyzes some of the motives for aggressive Southern expansionism in the 1850s. Steven Oates, *To Purge This Land with Blood* (1970) effectively introduces John Brown; Benjamin Quarles, *Allies for Freedom: Blacks and John Brown* (1970) surveys the African American relationship with Brown. No one interested in Brown can afford to overlook Bruce

Olds's unusually powerful historical novel, *Raising Holy Hell* (1995).

Racist aspects of free-soil ideology and the pre-war Republican Party are treated in Eugene Berwanger, *The Frontier Against Slavery* (1967). Michael Holt, *Forging a Majority: The Formation of the Republican Party in Pittsburgh, 1848–1860* (1969) and Ronald P. Formisano, *The Birth of Mass Political Parties: Michigan, 1827–1861* (1971) present different views of nativism and Republican politics from those developed in Tyler Anbinder, *Nativism and Slavery* (1992).

Several works make much-needed sense of Abraham Lincoln's views on slavery and race equality: George Fredrickson, "A Man but Not a Brother: Abraham Lincoln and Race Equality," *Journal of Southern History* (1975); Don E. Fehrenbacher, "Only His Stepchildren: Lincoln and the Negro," in George Fredrickson, ed., *A Nation Divided* (1975); and Mark Neeley, *Abraham Lincoln and the Promise of America: The Last Best Hope on Earth* (1993). A useful historiographical treatment of the causes of the Civil War is Thomas J. Pressley, *Americans Interpret Their Civil War* (1954), which should be supplemented with Eric Foner, "The Causes of the Civil War: Recent Interpretations and New Directions," in Foner, *Politics and Ideology in the Age of the Civil War* (1980).

8. TRIUMPH AND TRAGEDY: ABOLITIONISTS AND EMANCIPATION

A useful historiographical essay which considers abolitionism from the standpoint of Reconstruction is Richard O. Curry, "The Abolitionists and Reconstruction: A Critical Appraisal," *Journal of Southern History* (1968). James M. McPherson, *The Struggle for Equality: The Abolitionists and the Negro in the Civil War and Reconstruction* (1964) details immediatist activity from 1861 through the end of the decade. V. Jacques Voegli, *Free but Not Equal: The Negro in the Midwest during the Civil War and Reconstruction* (1967) and Forrest Wood, *Black Scare: The Racist Response to Emancipation and Reconstruction* (1970) both emphasize the continuity of white supremacism in Northern politics after 1861.

The most comprehensive modern view of Reconstruction is Eric Foner, *Reconstruction: America's Unfinished Revolution 1863– 1877* (1990). Black political activism, military participation, and other experiences during the Civil War and afterward can be followed in James M. McPherson, ed., *The Negro's Civil War* (1965); Benjamin Dudley Cornish, *The Sable Arm* (1956); Joseph Glatthaar, *Forged in Battle: The Civil War Alliance between Black Soldiers and White Officers* (1990); Peter Kolchin, *First Freedom: The Response of Alabama's Blacks to Emancipation and Reconstruction* (1972); Eric Foner, *Nothing but Freedom: Emancipation and Its Legacies* (1983); and Otis Singletary, *The Negro Militia and Reconstruction* (1957). The history of the Freedmen's Bureau is presented in William McFeeley, *Yankee Stepfather: General O. O. Howard and the Freedmen* (1968) and Martin Abbott, *The Freedmen's Bureau in South Carolina* (1967).

John Hope Franklin, ed., *The Emancipation Proclamation* (1963) traces the Republican Party's evolution to support of emancipation. Willie Lee Rose, *Rehearsal for Reconstruction: The Port Royal Experiment* (1964) and Joel Williamson, *After Slavery* (1965) offer many insights on the transition "from slavery to freedom." Rose's book also considers the war's impact on abolitionists, a topic also addressed in George Fredrickson, *The Inner Civil War: Northern Intellectuals and the Crisis of the Union* (1965).

For the politics of Reconstruction, the role of Andrew Johnson, and the limits of Republican radicalism, see Eric McKittrick, *Andrew Johnson and Reconstruction* (1960); Michael Les Benedict, *A Compromise of Principle* (1974); W. R. Brock, *An American Crisis: Congress and Reconstruction 1865–1867* (1963);

and C. Vann Woodward, "Seeds of Failure: The Radical Race Policy," in Harold Hyman, ed., *New Frontiers in Reconstruction* (1966). On the waning of Reconstruction, good general treatments are Vincent P. De Santis, *Republicans Face the Southern Question* (1959) and Stanley Hirshson, *Farewell to the Bloody Shirt* (1962). The links between abolitionism and later civil-rights movements are explored in James M. McPherson, *The Abolitionist Legacy: From Reconstruction to the NAACP* (1976). Finally, abolitionists are shown contemplating the ambiguous outcome of their crusade in Larry Gara, "A Glorious Time: The 1874 Abolitionist Reunion in Chicago," *Journal of the Illinois State Historical Society* (1972).

INDEX